Browne Roberts

History of the colonial empire of Great Britain

Browne Roberts

History of the colonial empire of Great Britain

ISBN/EAN: 9783337152666

Printed in Europe, USA, Canada, Australia, Japan

Cover: Foto ©ninafisch / pixelio.de

More available books at **www.hansebooks.com**

HISTORY

OF

THE COLONIAL EMPIRE

OF

GREAT BRITAIN

BY

BROWNE H. E. ROBERTS, B.A.

OF THE UNIVERSITY OF OXFORD

LONDON
LONGMAN, GREEN, LONGMAN, AND ROBERTS
1861

TO

A. A. ROBERTS, ESQ., C.B.

COMMISSIONER OF RAWUL PINDEE
AND OFFICIATING JUDICIAL COMMISSIONER OF THE PUNJAB.

My dear Brother,

I dedicate this little work to you, as a testimony of my sincere esteem and affection, and because I know the great interest you take in these subjects, and how zealous an advocate you are of the extension of useful knowledge generally in the community of your fellow-men.

Yours &c.

BROWNE ROBERTS.

London:
October 14, 1861

PREFACE.

THE Colonial Empire of Great Britain has now existed for so long a period, and has assumed such vast proportions, that some account of its origin, and of the various fluctuations to which it has been subjected in the progress of the last three centuries, cannot be otherwise than useful and, I hope, acceptable to the reading portion of our countrymen. The interests, moreover, of our colonies are so closely linked with those of the mother country, and they have become so essential a part of her riches and power, that the later history of England can never be properly appreciated without a competent knowledge of the subject. It is furthermore particularly to be desired that the younger portion of the community should early acquire some information of our colonial history, and of the local position, as well as of the relative importance, of the several possessions of the British Crown at the present time.

The term "colony" is one to which a very diverse interpretation has been given. I have not failed to give it a wide acceptance in the present work, as comprehending all the trans-marine possessions of our Crown, with the exception of the vast empire in Hindostan, a political phenomenon altogether without any equal either in contemporary or former history. Should the present work meet with a favourable reception, it is the intention of the author to bring out a companion to it in the shape of a "History of the British Empire in India."

EVERTON: September, 1861.

CONTENTS.

	Page
PREFACE	vii
INTRODUCTORY CHAPTER. — Sketch of the Rise and Progress of the Colonial Empire of Great Britain . .	1

SECTION I.

BRITISH NORTH AMERICA. — PART I.

CHAP. I. — Early History of the North American Colonies	18
„ II. — The American Revolution	29
„ III. — The American Revolution (*continued*) . .	42

SECTION II.

BRITISH NORTH AMERICA. — PART II.

CHAP. I. — History of Canada	53
„ II. — History of Canada from the Union . .	67
„ III. — History of Nova Scotia, Cape Breton Island, the Magdalen Islands, and Sable Island . .	73
„ IV. — History of New Brunswick, Prince Edward Island, Newfoundland, the Hudson's Bay Territory, and British Columbia	82

SECTION III.

THE WEST INDIES.

	Page
CHAP. I. — Discovery and Colonisation by European Nations	94
„ II. — History of Jamaica	101
„ III. — History of Jamaica. — Abolition of the Slave-trade. — Emancipation of the Negroes	114
„ IV. — Barbadoes. — The Windward Islands. — Trinidad	128
„ V. — The Leeward Islands	147
„ VI. — The Bahama and Bermuda Archipelagoes	161
„ VII. — Honduras and other Dependencies of Jamaica. — British Guiana. — General Remarks	166

SECTION IV.

AFRICA, AND ISLANDS OF THE ATLANTIC.

CHAP. I. — Progress of African Discovery; Settlements on the North-west Coast, and Remarks on the African Slave-trade	182
„ II. — The Gold Coast, and Islands in the Atlantic Ocean	195
„ III. — The Cape of Good Hope	203
„ IV. — The Cape of Good Hope (*continued*). — Port Natal	212

SECTION V.

REGIONS OF THE SOUTHERN OCEAN.

CHAP. I. — Australia. — Its Discovery and early History. — Colony of New South Wales	224
„ II. — History of Victoria, — of South Australia, — and of West Australia	233
„ III. — Tasmania. — Its History and Statistics	248

		Page
Chap. IV.—New Zealand. — Geographical Account and History		255
,, V. — History of New Zealand (*continued*) . .		273
,, VI. — Islands of the Southern Ocean. — Discovery of an Antarctic Continent. — The Falklands. — The Aucklands. — The Chatham Group . .		279

SECTION VI.

THE REMAINING BRITISH COLONIES.

Chap. I. — History of Ceylon, and of the Mauritius, or Isle of France		284
,, II. — Pulo Penang. — Malacca. — Singapore. — Hong-Kong. — Borneo and Sarawak. — Labuan		293
,, III. — History of Aden. — The Ionian Islands. — Gibraltar Heligoland. — Concluding Remarks . .		301

HISTORY

OF THE

COLONIAL EMPIRE OF GREAT BRITAIN.

INTRODUCTORY CHAPTER.

SKETCH OF THE RISE AND PROGRESS OF THE COLONIAL EMPIRE OF GREAT BRITAIN.

THE discovery of the great western continent of America, towards the close of the fifteenth century, by Christopher Columbus, is unquestionably one of the most remarkable events in the world's history; and the spirit of enterprise which at that period seized the minds of men in all parts of Europe, was but the natural consequence of the successful expeditions of that truly great man on the one hand, and on the other of those bold investigators who, about the same period, laid open to the curiosity and commercial enterprise of Western Christendom the passage round the Cape of Good Hope to India, and the rest of the Oriental

World.* Our own country, ever the nursing mother of brave seamen, was not long behindhand in availing herself of the opportunities thus opened for enterprise and adventure in the search of hitherto unknown regions. The English sovereign of that period, Henry the Seventh, has the honour of being among the greatest promoters of expeditions of this character, and it was under his patronage that John Cabot sailed on his celebrated voyage for the purpose of finding a north-western passage to Cathay or China, which was, however, rewarded instead by the discovery of the north-eastern coast of the American Continent, somewhere near the island of Newfoundland. He took formal possession of the territory in question in the name of the King of England, and on his return to this country received the honour of knighthood. In the year 1502 we have record of some design on the part of the English government to colonise this territory, which does not, however, appear to have had any practical effect whatever. Henry the Eighth sent out an expedition in 1527, with a view of discovering a north-western passage to the Pacific Ocean, which was attended with disastrous results. These early enterprises deserve notice, as being the first efforts towards the establishment of that great maritime

* Columbus discovered the western shore on the 12th Oct. A.D. 1492, Vasco de Gama rounded the Cape of Storms, since called the Cape of Good Hope, for the first time in A.D. 1479.

power, whose limits extend now to the most distant regions of the globe.

On the accession of Elizabeth, that illustrious monarch, who deserves more than any other to be called the founder of our national greatness and prosperity, did not fail to pay attention to these important subjects, and in 1576 she fitted out an expedition consisting of three ships, under the command of Martin Frobisher, for the purpose of exploring hitherto unknown regions. In this and several subsequent voyages of Frobisher, valuable discoveries were made. In 1579, another attempt towards the colonisation of the north-eastern coast of America was made under the patronage of the Queen, who granted a patent to Sir Humphrey Gilbert "for the discovering or occupying and peopling such remote, heathen, and barbarous countries as were not actually possessed by any Christian people." Gilbert, who appears to have been a man of great energy and moral courage, led forth two expeditions for the purpose thus specified, the second of which was crowned with success for a brief period, a settlement being made in the island of Newfoundland, which, however, was abandoned in the first years of the succeeding century.

We have hitherto had to record enterprises of but small result as far as the establishment of colonies and the progress of national wealth is concerned; towards the close of Elizabeth's reign, however, a most important step was made in our colonial history by the establishment, as a corporate body, of certain adventurers under the title of "the Governor and Company of Merchants of London trading in the East Indies."

This event took place in the year 1600, the Queen having hesitated for some time to grant the charter of incorporation from apprehension of giving offence to the Spanish government. The charter was originally intended to last for fifteen years only, but in 1609, it was rendered perpetual, with this saving clause, that should any national detriment be at any time found to ensue, these exclusive privileges should expire after three years notice. By it, the East India Company obtained the right of purchasing lands without limitation, with the monopoly of their trade under the direction of a governor and twenty-four other persons in committee, to be elected annually. The first establishments made by the company in the east for the purpose of carrying on their trade, were at Surat on the western coast of Hindostan, and at Bantam in the island of Java.

The first of all our colonies to obtain a charter, was Virginia, in the North American continent. This settlement was originally planned by Sir Walter Raleigh in 1583, and named in honour of Queen Elizabeth, who extended her patronage to the scheme. Raleigh's attempts to colonise that country were, however, unsuccessful, and the first regular settlement in

Virginia, was made in 1607, after the accession of James the First to the English throne.

The foundation of many of our colonies in the West Indies, in North America, and on the western coast of Africa, date from that active period of English history, the early part of the seventeenth century. Barbadoes was founded in 1624, and Bermuda in 1609; the Bahama Islands in 1672; Antigua, Montserrat, and St. Christophers in 1632; while the large, fertile, and beautiful island of Jamaica, was captured by England from Spain in 1655. The religious and political dissensions of the mother country at that period contributed in a remarkable manner to the development of our colonial empire. In 1620, a band of the puritans, in order to rid themselves of the persecution to which they were subjected by the government and the established church in England, determined upon leaving their native country for ever to seek some distant shore, where they might enjoy perfect freedom of conscience, and celebrate their own form of worship without molestation. Accordingly, the Pilgrim Fathers, as they have been styled by the veneration of after ages, steered their course westward in a single ship, and finally anchored on the shores of Massachusetts, where they laid the foundation of the state which still bears that name. They were followed by others of their religious persuasion, by whom were founded in rapid succession the other "New England" states, as they are called, namely, New Hampshire, Connecticut, and Rhode Island; North and South Carolina were established between the years 1650-70; Pennsylvania in 1602; and New York was conquered from the Dutch in 1674. Of our present North American colonies, Nova Scotia was established in 1621, and Newfoundland in 1623. In 1670 a charter was granted to a certain body of men under the title of the "Hudson's Bay Company," together with the power of exercising authority over a large territory in the extreme north of the American continent. Settlements were made and forts established by the British government on the Gambia (river) and the Gold Coast of Africa between the years 1618 and 1631. Fort William was established on the site of the present city of Calcutta in 1656, and Bombay Island was settled in 1661.

In the year 1704, the great fortress of Gibraltar was captured from Spain by the English. In 1759 the important settlement of Canada was taken from the French, and has since remained a British colony. St. Vincents, Tobago, Grenada, and Dominica were captured from the same power in 1763. Prince Edward Island was colonised by settlers from this country in 1771, and New Brunswick in 1764. Pulo Penang, on the coast of the Malayan Peninsula, was made a British settlement in 1786, and Sierra Leone on the western coast of Africa in 1787. In the same year,

1787, were made the first attempts towards the colonisation of the vast territory of Australia, by the formation of the settlement of New South Wales. The Andaman Islands were captured in 1793, and Ceylon, previously a Dutch possession, in 1795. Trinidad, a Spanish settlement, was captured in 1797. Malta was taken out of the hands of the French in 1800: and in the same year a settlement was made in the small Island of Penin, at the entrance of the Red Sea.

Van Dieman's Land, or Tasmania, was first colonised in 1803, and in the same year Guiana and St. Lucia became British territories. The Dutch settlement at the Cape of Good Hope in south Africa, was captured by a British force in 1806. The Islands of Mauritius and Seychelles in the Indian Ocean were taken from the French in 1800, and the Ionian Islands on the western coast of Greece about the same time. Singapore became a British settlement in 1819, Malacca in 1826, and Aden in 1838.

Of our Australian colonies, Western Australia was founded in 1829; Southern Australia in 1834-5; Port Philip in 1835; and New Zealand in 1839. A settlement was made in the Falkland Islands in 1841. Hong-Kong was captured from the Chinese government in 1842-3. The province of Natal, on the south-west coast of Africa, was made a British colony in 1844. The island of Labuan, off the coast of Borneo, was settled by the English in 1847; and Vancouver's Island, on the north-west coast of America, in 1848 ; while British Columbia, on the west of the North American continent, was declared a colony of Great Britain in 1858.

Our colonial history is not, however, one entirely of victory, conquest, or the peaceful formation of new settlements, though it seemed best not to interrupt the foregoing narrative by detailing incidents of a different bearing. It becomes the duty of the historian now, however, to record the greatest disaster which has ever befallen the empire of Great Britain, in the disruption by violence of the greater part of our North American colonies from their mother country. As it is intended in the after part of this work to enter more fully into that subject, a sketch of the principal circumstances of the revolt of the United States, and their subsequent war of independence, will suffice for the present. The first cause of a serious difference between the old and new countries was the attempt of Mr. George Grenville, as Prime Minister of England, to impose a tax on the American colonies through the medium of the British Parliament. As the Americans had not any representatives in the home legislature, they denied the right of that body to tax them. The imperial government unfortunately did not give to their appeals on this subject the hearing to which they were entitled from their general justice and moderation in the first instance, and both sides adhering to their previous opinions with the same firmness, as they perceived their opponents becoming more and more obstinate and fierce in their hostility, in a few years open war broke out on the American continent, a war which even the near relationship of the two countries engaged in it, could not prevent from being of a sanguinary and disastrous character. The United Colonies, or States, as they were now called, having elected a parliament of their own for the purposes of legislation, this body passed a decree on the 4th of July, 1776, declaring their country independent, and constituting a republican form of government among themselves. Their independence was ere long recognised by the governments of France and Spain, those two countries entering eagerly into the contest against Great Britain. The final result of the war was the recognition of American independence by this country also; a treaty of peace being concluded to that effect at Versailles, on the 3rd September, 1783. Upon this war the resources of our country had been poured forth with a lavish hand, and its termination left her in a state of great exhaustion, with her most bitter enemies exulting on all hands at her temporary humiliation. This exultation, however, was amply compensated for a few years after, in the calamities both of France and Spain; the former of these countries having learnt, from contact with America, those revolutionary principles which soon deluged her own soil with blood, and the latter experiencing an equally prejudicial effect in the loss of her South American colonies, which were not long in following the example of independence given them by their brethren of the north.

The great contest in which this country became engaged towards the close of the last century, in the first instance with revolutionary France alone, but ultimately with entire Europe marshalled under the banner of the great Napoleon, was attended with very prosperous results, in so far as the growth of her colonial empire was concerned. In the progress of this great war, nearly every one of the trans-marine possessions of France was wrested from that power by the combined efforts of the army and navy of Great Britain; and so vast were the dimensions of the latter empire in consequence, and such a variety of resources was comprised within its boundaries, that she felt but few serious effects from the decrees issued by Napoleon in 1806-7, at Berlin and Milan, by which that keen-sighted statesman endeavoured to accomplish her ruin, by excluding her from all commercial intercourse with the continent of Europe. "I must have ships, colonies, and commerce," was the imperious declaration of the first Napoleon; that most important end, which he desired mainly for the sake of humiliating this country, was not, however, successfully accomplished by France until many years after. Under the rule of

Napoleon the Third, and by the pursuit of quite an opposite system of policy, France has acquired almost more than her former naval pre-eminence; her colonial possessions are once more found side by side with those of England, in many parts of the globe; while she has seized upon a vast territory in Northern Africa, which though requiring enormous expenditure on her part for its maintenance as a French colony, has added not a little to her military superiority of late years, from the bravery and intrepidity of the regiments which it has contributed to the army of France. These are facts which may well occupy the attention of every thoughtful person, as showing the superior wisdom of a pacific policy between great and enlightened countries, and those who direct their interest, over that which history has revealed, according to whose records nations seem to have studied the art of mutual destruction rather than a happy rivalry in profitable industry and the arts of peace.

During the half century which has now almost elapsed, since the conclusion of the great European war, England has profited not a little from the more pacific state of the world generally, to foster the growth of her numerous colonies, and attend to the development of the various resources contained within their boundaries. Seconded as she has been moreover by the enterprise and industry of her own sons, it may fairly be said that results have been achieved such as for greatness and variety have never before been accomplished in so brief a period. A few remarks will suffice to place before the reader a general view of these important facts. The population of Canada, which at the time of its conquest from the French in 1760 numbered only 65,000 inhabitants, at the present time, in its two provinces of Upper and Lower Canada, amounts to about 2,000,000, including a mixture of British emigrants, settlers from the United States, and the descendants of the original French colonists, with a few Indians. Of the other North American colonies, Nova Scotia, which in 1764 contained 13,000 inhabitants only, in 1817 contained 84,000, and at present consists of about 300,000; Cape Breton Island contained in 1849, 49,600 inhabitants; New Brunswick contained in 1783, 11,457; in 1848 its estimated population was 208,012; Prince Edward Island numbered in 1802, 20,651, in 1849 about 55,000; in 1785 the population of Newfoundland was 10,224, at present it is upwards of 100,000. The entire population of British North America may at present be estimated at 3,000,000.

The first attempt, as already stated, to make a settlement in Australia was in the year 1788, when a penal colony was established at Port Jackson in New South Wales. At the present time that magnificent country is peopled by about half-a-million of European settlers, distributed in the following manner: New

South Wales contained in 1848, 220,474 white inhabitants; South Australia, which was founded between 1834-36, contained in 1850 an estimated population of about 50,000 whites; West Australia was founded in 1829-30, and, in 1848, contained 4622 white inhabitants; Victoria, hitherto the most prosperous of all our Australian colonies, was founded in 1835, and since the discovery of gold there in 1849-50, its population has increased with extraordinary rapidity; in 1850 it was estimated at 50,000.

Van Dieman's Island, now known by the name of Tasmania, was first made a British settlement in 1803; in 1848 its population, including a large proportion of convicts, amounted to 74,741.

New Zealand was made subject to the authority of the British Crown in the year 1840, after a severe contest with the native inhabitants; in 1844 it already numbered a white population of 11,948.

The Cape Colony in southern Africa was conquered by British arms from the Dutch in the year 1795, but was restored to its former owners by the Treaty of Amiens. On the renewal of the war it was again occupied by a British force in 1806, and has since remained a valuable appanage of the British Crown. Its present population is estimated at about 300,000.

Great Britain also possesses settlements on the northwest coast of Africa, at the mouth of the river Gambia, and at Sierra Leone. These settlements were originally acquired and maintained principally for the purpose of stimulating and profiting by the infamous slave traffic; their chief value and importance is now, perhaps, derived from the fact that they serve as military and naval stations for our government in its untiring efforts to suppress that odious system. Great Britain also possesses a territory on the Gold Coast amounting to some 280 miles in length, the negro population in which amounts to about 300,000. Much may be hoped from this and our other possessions on the African coast, on account of the good influence exercised through their means in civilising that dense population which lies imbedded in the interior of that vast continent, and which has now for ages been sunk in the lowest condition of mental and social degradation of which humanity is capable.

A rebellion broke out in Canada in the year 1837, and another in the following year, 1838; both, however, proved very partial movements, and, being altogether resisted by the better class of the population in that country, were without much difficulty quelled. England has, indeed, learnt a terrible lesson from the manner in which the United States became severed from her, and she has not failed since that period to extend to the inhabitants of all her colonies such rights and privileges as place them on a level with those of the mother country, and leave little room for disaffection from any but the factious and evil-minded. Each of her colonies, on arriving at a sufficient maturity, is now provided with a representative assembly elected by the inhabitants, and a legislative council nominated by the Crown, the whole being presided over by a governor, appointed in like manner by the Crown, and who is the representative of the sovereign. This functionary, as well as all the principal officials in the several colonies, is nominated by the colonial secretary of the Crown, who is always a member of the British Cabinet. The Imperial Parliament has authority to suspend the legislature of any one of the colonies, as well as to alter, abridge, or extend its functions; it also claims the right to interfere in the taxation of such of the colonies as do not possess a parliamentary government of their own. The House of Lords is, moreover, the supreme court before which any colonial governor or other high functionary is brought for trial after impeachment by the House of Commons.

It is scarcely to be expected that the British colonies will for ever remain dependencies of this great empire. As they attain the full growth of nations they will doubtless be prepared to claim for themselves an entire right of self-government. One hope, may, however be confidently expressed: that whensoever that time shall come, they will not separate in anger, but with thorough good-will on either side, and with feelings of fraternal esteem and attachment which no time shall alter or impair.

A very important effect has been produced in the progress of our colonies by the discovery of gold fields within the last ten years, first in the Australian colony of Victoria, and afterwards in the territory of British Columbia on the north-west coast of the American continent. The consequence of these discoveries has been a great rush of immigrants from every part of the world, the Chinaman being found at the gold "diggings" side by side with the members of every nation of Europe, as well as the ardent sons of America. As might reasonably be expected these recently formed communities present a strange social aspect, not unaccompanied by frequent outrages perpetrated by the settlers on one another, which there does not appear to have been hitherto any authority at hand to repress, the government being, indeed, practically in the hands of the immigrants themselves. These are evils which we may confidently look for time and the gradual progress of events in these settlements to correct; and in the meanwhile great advantages have resulted to the world in general from the discovery of the gold fields and the impetus given thereby to industry and commercial enterprise everywhere, while the growth of our colonial empire in Australia and North America has been wonderfully promoted thereby.

Meanwhile in the far off shores of the Fraser River

we seem to have reached at last the " Ultima Thule " of colonial enterprise; henceforth the efforts, both of rulers and people, will in all probability be directed chiefly to the development of the *internal* resources of the British possessions in every habitable part of the globe.

SECTION I.

BRITISH NORTH AMERICA.—PART I.

CHAPTER I.

EARLY HISTORY OF THE NORTH AMERICAN COLONIES.

HAVING previously related how the great North American continent became first tenanted by British settlers, we will here give a brief description of the aboriginal tribes whom they found already in possession of the soil there. It has been well said that "the character of these tribes has been most differently portrayed, sometimes invested with imaginery virtues from a vague admiration of savage life, sometimes to justify oppression loaded with as imaginary crimes. It will be found, that in general they are painted all bright in poetry and all black in state papers. In truth, they might often be admired for generous and lofty feelings, but were ever liable to be swayed to and fro by any sudden impulse, by their passions or their wants. They would endure bodily torment with the most heroic courage, and inflict it with the most unrelenting cruelty. Whenever they had neither warfare nor the chase in view they seemed indolent, dissolute and listless, yet always with an inborn dignity of demeanour and a peculiar picturesqueness of language. In hostilities, on the contrary, they were found most formidable from their skilful and stealthy marches, their unforeseen attacks, and their ferocity in slaying and scalping their opponents."* On the whole, these savage tribes would appear to have been not very far removed in the scale of humanity from the barbarians whom the first and greatest of the Cæsars found ranged along the coast of Britain on his first attempt to land there. Like them, the Red Indians of America went about almost or entirely naked, and dyed their bodies in a manner that sometimes showed considerable ingenuity; like them they lived either in holes and caves of the earth, or in wigwams rudely constructed of unhewn timber with a hole above to let in light and admit the escape of air; and, finally, striking similarity is displayed in the circumstance that in both countries the scale of civilisation and the arts of social life seems to have declined as the traveller proceeded farther north that the equator.

Our countrymen, however, professed to invade America in a very different spirit from that in which

* Lord Mahon's " Hist. of England," vol. v. p. 79.

the Romans had come of old to their own shores. Instead of conquest and plunder, they announced their simple intention to found settlements on the soil, and for this purpose signed treaties with the native tribes. In some cases a higher object was proclaimed by them, the conversion of these poor savages to the blessings of Christianity. Thus, for instance, the seal of the colony of Massachusetts bore an Indian erect, with an arrow in his right hand, and the motto " Come over and help us." * That our countrymen were originally sincere in the expression of that simple and irreproachable object we ought not perhaps to doubt; the result of their endeavours has, nevertheless, proved a disastrous one, as far as the Red Indian tribes have been concerned. The attempts to convert them to Christianity, at least on the part of Protestants, have met with very little success.† On the other hand, they have rushed most eagerly on the temptation offered them by Europeans in the shape of ardent liquors, and so utterly demoralising have been the results of this fatal propensity, that their whole race seems to be rapidly disappearing from the face of the earth.

Virginia, as has been before stated, was the oldest of

---

* Bancroft's "Hist. of the United States," vol. i. p. 346, ed. 1839.

† There seems no doubt but that the missionaries of Rome have been more successful with the American Indians, perhaps from the circumstance that their religion, being more addressed to the senses, is more easily comprehended by the untutored mind of the savage.

our North American colonies. In 1607, the design which had been earlier entertained in the fertile brain of Sir Walter Raleigh, of colonising the territory bordering on the shore of the river Potomac, was first actually carried into execution, under the somewhat unwilling auspices (it has been hinted) of King James the First, who foresaw the extension of liberal ideas among the settlers in the boundless territories of the far west. The colony does not appear to have prospered or extended much beyond its original bounds, until a change was brought about by the introduction of negro slaves for the purpose of labouring in its plantations. The slave trade on the coast of Nigritia and other countries of Central Africa inhabited by the Ethiopian, or negro race, had already become a fixed principle, and had attained vast proportions among the Christian nations of southern Europe, and the Mohammedan tribes of the north of Africa before the date of the discovery of America by Columbus. It was not long after that event that the Spanish settlers in the New World, particularly in the island of Hispaniola, began to import negro slaves from Africa to labour on the soil, and in the mines of the newly-discovered territory. At first this movement is said to have had the patronage of those whose only motive could be and was benevolence towards their brother men. Las Casas, an excellent missionary, on observing that a negro was

capable of enduring four times as much labour as the
native Indians: and that the latter race appeared
unsuited to severe toil of any kind, warmly advocated
the continued transportation of black labourers into
Hispaniola, and memorialised the home government of
Spain on this subject in the year 1517. The consequence
was that ere long, the West Indies began to
teem with a numerous population of negroes, which
multiplied with alarming fertility and has since produced
the most important effects on that portion of the
world.

The first importation of negroes into the colony of
Virginia took place in the year 1620, a cargo of them
being brought to its shores in a Dutch man-of-war.
"For many years," says the American historian, Mr.
Bancroft, "the Dutch were principally concerned in
the slave trade in the market of Virginia; the immediate
demand for labourers may, in part, have blinded
the eyes of the planters to the ultimate evils of slavery,
though the laws of the colony at a very early period
discouraged its increase by a special tax upon female
slaves." *

Some twenty-five years after the foundation of the
colony of New England, an attempt was made by

---

* Bancroft's "Hist. of the United States," vol. i. chap. v. This little
sketch of the rise of American slavery, as well as other valuable facts,
are drawn from the first volume of that great work; a volume, of which
it may be fairly said, that it is "worth its weight in gold."

some of the citizens of Massachusetts to introduce a cargo of negroes into the country. So indignant, however, were the descendants of the pilgrim fathers at "the heinous crime of man stealing," that the authors of the offence were committed, and the poor negroes were restored at the public expense to their native country. Indeed, to their honour, be it said that the inhabitants of that noble colony, seem at no time to have allowed the abominable system of slavery to be thoroughly introduced among them. In the words of the American historian, "the law (against slavery) was not enforced, but the principle lived among the people." On the whole, little or no blame can be attached to the settlers of our early colonies with regard to the introduction of negro slavery; the fact being pretty well beyond dispute, that this heinous system, and the slave trade by which it was fostered, were not prohibited by the law, and certainly formed part of the general policy of the mother country at the period in question.*

The colony of Maryland received its name from Henrietta Maria, the queen of Charles the First, and was founded in the year 1634, by Lord Baltimore, who being a Catholic, had induced others of his creed to join with him in transporting themselves to a country where they might hope to enjoy that freedom

* Mahon, vol. v. p. 77.

of conscience, which was denied them in the mother country. It is, moreover, greatly to their honour, that in constituting their infant community after their arrival in the noble bay of Chesapeake, they not only asserted liberty of conscience for themselves, but likewise granted it to the members of all other religious communities which acknowledge the doctrine of the Trinity, beyond that point their liberality did not extend. This is the first instance on record of any Christian community, in which even this limited extent of religious freedom was conceded.

In 1663, shortly after the restoration of Charles the Second, a scheme was set in hand by several English noblemen and gentlemen, among whom Monk, Duke of Albermarle, was the nominal head, for planting a great colony in the territory south of Virginia. Accordingly the country called Carolina, in honour of the king, was fixed upon, and Lord Shaftesbury, who was the active manager, set to work with the assistance of John Locke, the great writer on philosophy, to frame a constitution for the intended community, which, it was pompously announced, was to last for ever. Instead of this result, however, the new constitution does not appear so have been at any period established effectually, for the site of the new colony was already occupied by a small settlement of our countrymen who, having hitherto governed themselves, and framed such laws and regulations as their condition required, were indisposed to submit to the absolute authority of a junta of noblemen and gentlemen residing in England, whose only purpose was apparently to gratify their own avarice and ambition. The consequence was a long contest between the inhabitants of the colony and the "Proprietaries," as they were called, which terminated eventually in the establishment of a popular system of government. This colony, afterwards divided into North and South Carolina, proved a timely place of refuge for some of the Huguenots who were expelled from France in 1685, by the bigotry of the heartless tyrant Louis the Fourteenth, in his revocation of the Edict of Nantes.

The colony of New York was originally a Dutch settlement, established about the year 1625, under the name of New Netherlands. It does not appear to have been in a very flourishing condition during that period, the Dutch not possessing so happy a faculty as our countrymen in establishing free and representative institutions in their colonies. America, however, it has been judiciously observed, has had the peculiar good fortune to secure the representative institutions of England, while it was from Holland, that she borrowed the idea of federal union. In the course of the wars between this country and Holland during the reign of Charles the Second, the colony of New Netherlands became a British possession, and was called New York in honour of the king's brother, the Duke of York and Albany. From that period it remained a thriving dependency of the British crown, until the time of separation arrived.

New Jersey had belonged originally to the Dutch settlement of New Netherlands, but was sold by the Duke of York to Lord Berkeley and Sir George Cauteret. It speedily became the refuge of numbers of Nonconformists, who were glad to escape from the thraldom to which they were still subjected in England. The east and west portions of the colony, at first separate, were united under the same governor, council, and house of assembly in the reign of Queen Anne.

The state of Delaware receives its name from Lord Delaware, governor of the American possessions of England in the early part of the seventeenth century. The territory, which still retains this name, was colonised by Swedes about the year 1638, but ere long passed from their hands into those of the Dutch, and ultimately was transferred with New Netherlands to the British Crown. It appears to have been regarded subsequently in the light of an appendage to the state of Pennsylvania, and thus remained until the period of separation.

It was in the year 1682 that William Penn led a band of Quakers to take possession of that magnificent territory beyond the Delaware river, which was named by Charles the Second himself Pennsylvania, in honour of its first proprietary.* The spot fixed upon for their first rude settlement on the river Schuylkill, was the site of the magnificent city of Philadelphia. Thus did a plain English country gentleman, for such was Penn originally, suddenly become the founder and administrator of a fine territory.

This colony rose rapidly in population, wealth, and general importance; the Quakers, who remained for long the majority among its inhabitants, being, however, often considerably embarrassed when they were asked to contribute their portion towards the wars which were from time to time carried on by the imperial government. They satisfied their conscience on these occasions by voting sums of money "for the King's use," and not making any enquiry as to the purpose to which it might be applied.

Georgia, the latest in foundation of all these colonies, derived its name from George the Second, its real founder being General Oglethorpe, who, aided by some men of influence, set in hand this new colony with the benevolent intention of making it a place of refuge for insolvent debtors at home and persecuted Protestants abroad. The royal charter, which they obtained in 1732, declares that they sought the grant of the territory not for themselves, but in trust for the

---

* "Proprietary." This was the appellation given to those on whom the chief right of property, and also of government, in a new colony was conferred.

poor, and their motto was " Non sibi sed aliis." The growth of the infant colony was nourished by a large immigration of Moravians. It should be mentioned, moreover, to the honour of its founders, that the introduction of negro slaves was not permitted so long as their influence prevailed.

CHAP. II.

THE AMERICAN REVOLUTION.

At a short period after the treaty of Paris in 1762-3, the population of the thirteen colonies, which were destined to become the United States of North America, has been estimated at two millions of European descent, about half a million of negroes, and a sprinkling of the old aboriginal tribes. It has been shown that these colonies differed from one another very much in the purposes for which they were originally founded, and also in the character of those who were their first settlers. Besides their original differences, there were jealousies and heart-burnings from time to time arising among them on commercial and financial subjects. The thoughtful reader can, therefore, scarcely come to ny other conclusion than that it must have been some matter of profound importance, indeed, which could have, as it were, in a moment of time, healed so many jarring interests, and cause the whole continent from the Gulf of Mexico to the Gulf of St. Lawrence to combine in one bold attitude of defiance to the mother country. The following is a narrative of these events.

The American colonies had always been accustomed to yield their portion to the general revenue of the empire; and this they performed by a vote of their provincial assemblies at the requisition of the British government. Shortly after the peace of Paris in 1763, however, it struck Mr. George Grenville, then first minister of the crown, that as the late war had been carried on in great measure for the benefit of our American colonies, it was but fair that they should be called upon to bear part of the burden; and he determined to effect this object by means of certain stamp duties, to be imposed on the Americans by the authority of the British parliament. A resolution to this effect was accordingly carried through both houses attracting little notice at the moment in England.

Very different was the manner in which the news was received across the Atlantic. The colonies were almost unanimous in the serious opinion they expressed upon the subject; they took their stand upon the broad fact that as Englishmen they were entitled to an equality of rights with the inhabitants of the mother country, and could not be taxed by a vote of the House of Commons, in which assembly they were altogether unrepresented. At the same time they expressed their utmost readiness to contribute to the common expenses of the empire in the manner they had always been accustomed to do, namely by a vote of their provincial assemblies. Instead of paying attention to these remonstrances, Mr. Grenville in the session of 1765 proceeded to pass through Parliament the bill, of which he had given notice, imposing certain stamp duties on the American colonies, a measure which was not then thought of much importance at home.

When, however, the intelligence of this proceeding reached the shores of North America, the excitement and consternation were very great there. At Boston the flags of ships in the harbour were raised half-mast high, and the church bells tolled as for some great public calamity; while similar demonstrations took place in the other large cities. The provincial assemblies passed resolutions denying the right of the mother country to tax them without their own consent, and took a bolder step in sending delegates to a general congress, which was to meet at New York in a few months time, and take measures for the general safety of the colonies. It would have been well had the Americans paused there, but from remonstrances they soon proceeded to outrages, and the principle towns across the Atlantic became a constant scene of riot and confusion.

By the time that the news of these startling occurrences had reached England, the minister to whose arrogant and short-sighted policy they must chiefly be attributed had resigned, and his place was supplied by the Marquis of Rockingham and General Conway. The new ministers passed amid general applause a measure repealing the Stamp Act, but at the same time the general authority of Parliament over the colonies in all matters of legislation was asserted in another bill. These measures certainly gave great satisfaction in America, but matters by no means regained their former footing between the two countries; and there appears to have been a strong party on the other side of the Atlantic, who, from the first, were resolved upon separation from the mother country and the establishment of a republican form of government.

No event of any great importance appears to have taken place after this between England and her colonies until the year 1767, when Mr. Townshend, as Chancellor of the Exchequer, proposed certain small taxes on glass, paper, painters' colours, and tea, to be paid as import duties by the Americans. Dr. Franklin, who was residing in London as agent from the colony of Massachusetts, had formerly acknowledged a distinction between internal taxation and customs duties, or external taxation, admitting the right of the British Parliament to impose the latter but not the former on the colonies. He now, however, retracted his former statements, finding his countrymen generally most keenly opposed to the idea of being taxed *at all* without their own consent. On the arrival at Boston of the news that further measures for their taxation were in contemplation, or already passed, the Assembly of that province in February, 1768, addressed a circular letter to the other American provinces calling upon them to combine in measures of defence. Shortly afterwards some riotous proceedings took place at Boston, upon which the Secretary of State for the Colonies, Lord Hillsborough, ordered a detachment of the army to take up their quarters in that city, greatly to the disgust of its inhabitants. An association styling themselves " the sons of liberty " was speedily formed among the colonies, the members of which pledged themselves not to make use of any articles imported from England. In the year 1770 a very serious affray took place between the mob at Boston and the soldiers quartered there, whose presence had from the first been most obnoxious to the townspeople; in this encounter several lives were lost on the part of the people. The mob had also begun to maltreat there and elsewhere all who where suspected of being secret adherents to the English government.

In the year 1773, was passed through the British Parliament a measure, which led to the final estrangement of the two countries, and to a sanguinary struggle between them. This measure was to all appearance of an insignificant character, consisting in the withdrawal of certain duties on tea shipped by the agents of the East India Company from England to America; and the object of the government in passing it, was to lend a helping hand to that company, whose financial affairs were then in a very unsatisfactory condition. During the summer of that year, the company freighted several vessels with tea for the American colonies, and appointed agents in each colony to dispose of the cargo on its arrival.

Meanwhile, the English government having taken offence at the conduct of Dr. Franklin, that gentleman was informed that the King had no further occasion for his services as Deputy-Postmaster-General for the Colonies. This dismissal was deeply resented in America, where Franklin was at that time the idol of the people, being regarded as the most prominent and illustrious defender of their common liberties. On the arrival of the ships laden with tea at the different ports of North America, the popular indignation there rose to its highest pitch, and speedily burst into a flame. A number of persons disguised as Mohawk Indians, boarded the ships which anchored thus laden in Boston harbour, and scattered the contents of them into the water. On the 4th September, 1774, a general congress of deputies sent by twelve of the American colonies*, met at Philadelphia; they conducted their business in secret, and with apparent unanimity.

On intelligence of these events reaching England,

---

* Georgia joined the rest subsequently, and completed the original number of thirteen " United States."

very general indignation was expressed, the proceedings of the Americans being considered of a totally unwarrantable character. The Earl of Chatham, in concurrence with Dr. Franklin, framed a measure which was intended as a basis of reconciliation between the two countries. This measure, which was of a bold and comprehensive character, worthy of the great statesman from whom it emanated in the first instance, was introduced into the House of Lords by the earl on the 1st February, 1775.

Neither Houses of Parliament were in the humour for listening to any scheme of conciliation, and the consequence was that Lord Chatham's bill was rejected in a very summary manner by a large majority. A few weeks afterwards, resolutions of a similar character, brought forward by Mr. Burke, were negatived by a very large majority of the House of Commons.

Both countries now began to prepare for that trial of arms which seemed inevitable. Dr. Franklin arrived in America on the 5th May, 1775, and was immediately chosen one of the deputies of Pennsylvania in the Congress which had been appointed to meet on the 10th day of that month. Before that time, however, the first blood had been shed between the sons of England and America; a battle being fought at Lexington, near Boston, between the colonists and a party of soldiers sent by General Gage to seize some American stores and ammunition. These soldiers were assailed at every step by unseen enemies from behind walls and other defences, and they returned, after having accomplished their object, with sadly diminished numbers. On the 10th May, a party of above three hundred men seized the forts of Ticonderoga and Crown Point, near Lake Champlain, and contrived to possess themselves of a sloop belonging to the royal navy on that lake. General Gage soon found himself quite besieged in the town of Boston, and, not having received the reinforcements promised from England, his position there had become somewhat perilous.

The Congress met according to their original appointment, on the 10th May at Philadelphia, and assumed as their title, " The United Colonies." They undertook to raise a loan in order to pay the expenses of the war on which they were entering, and made choice of a commander-in-chief in the person of General George Washington, whose appointment to that momentous office took place on the 15th June, 1775. The character of this truly great and good man has been too often portrayed to require much further tribute from these pages, suffice it then to say, that in making this appointment the American Congress might be supposed to have registered the decree of a beneficent Providence, so happy was it in its results to themselves and their posterity.

Ere the new commander-in-chief had time to reach the principal force of Americans collected round the city of Boston, a most important blow had been struck. The colonists had on the 16th June occupied an eminence overlooking the town, and General Gage, seeing its importance as a military position, determined to dispossess them of it. He accordingly dispatched a force of some 2000 men, who made several desperate attempts to gain the position; it was bravely defended by the colonists, and but for a timely reinforcement the royal troops would perhaps have been worsted in the encounter. As it was, they succeeded eventually in driving the Americans from their position, though the fruits of their victory were barren in the extreme. Such was the battle of Bunker's Hill, the sad commencement of this war between men of one language, one blood, and one religion!

As the breach between the two countries became widened, there had been an increasing desire on the part of the Americans to declare themselves independent of the British crown, and to establish a republican form of government. This movement made rapid progress from the commencement of the year 1776, during the earlier months of which several of the provinces separately declared themselves free of allegiance for the future to the mother country. At length on the 4th July of that year, the draft of a declaration of independence having been framed by a committee of the General Congress at Philadelphia, that body solemnly proclaimed the independence of its country, stating at length the reasons which had compelled it to that course. "From that day," say the American writers, "the word *Colonies* is not known in their history;"* they henceforth styled themselves the United States of America.

In the course of the summer of 1776 the English army evacuated Boston, and having been reinforced from home by General Howe, who now assumed the chief command, invaded New York during the month of August. Washington had been beforehand with them, however, and they found both the city itself and the neighbouring Long Island garrisoned by the Americans. On the 27th of August a sharp engagement took place on Long Island, which ended in the serious discomfiture of the Americans, and ere long New York itself was evacuated by their troops. The English were very successful for several months after this, and entertained hopes of winning back to the royal cause the provinces of New York and New Jersey, in both of which the "Tories" or loyal subjects of the crown were believed to be very numerous. The ground which Washington had lost was, however, pretty well recovered by that great man towards the close of the year. On Christmas day by a night march he surprised the British army at Trenton, and made the greater part of them prisoners. Another successful action at Princetown early in the new year (1777) quite

* Sparke's "Life of Washington," p. 182.

turned the scale of fortune, and revived the drooping spirits of the Americans.

. During the summer of this year Sir William Howe made a successful campaign on the river Delaware, and succeeded in capturing the important city of Philadelphia. Washington, who was opposed to Sir William in this campaign, gives from time to time lamentable accounts of the state of insubordination in his army, and the sadprivati ons to which they were reduced, being in many cases almost in want of clothes entirely, without blankets during the severity of winter, and with a dreadful scarcity of provisions. General Burgoyne about the same time invaded the United States from Canada, and advanced towards Albany on the Hudson river, where he expected to be joined by a detachment of the royal army from New York under the command of Sir Henry Clinton. Clinton's force failed to arrive at the looked for period, and Burgoyne was so pressed and harassed by a greatly superior force of Americans under the command of General Gates, that after holding a council of war with his principal officers, he resolved on making what he termed a " Convention of War," in fact a capitulation. He accordingly entered into negociations with General Gates, which resulted in a convention being signed on the 17th of October at Saratoga, according to which the British troops were to pile their arms, and then be marched through the enemy's country to the sea coast, whence they were as soon as possible to be embarked for England, on giving promise that they would not serve again in North America during the war that was being then waged. It is to be regretted that the American government did not faithfully carry out the terms of this convention; but contrived under various pretexts to detain the greater part of the capitulated force as prisoners of war several years in America.

The Convention of Saratoga has generally been regarded as the turning point in the war of American Independence. The colonists had for some time past been very depressed, and their cause was looked upon by foreign countries generally as at the last ebb, when this great piece of good fortune suddenly arrived to change the aspect of affairs entirely, and make their cause triumphant and secure. When the news reached Europe, at the close of the year 1777, the French government determined to recognise the independence of America, and furthermore to enter upon an alliance with that country. The people of France had from the first displayed great sympathy with the American cause, and many French officers, among whom was the Marquis de la Fayette, had gone over to offer their services to the Congress, which had accepted them thankfully, and had appointed them to high commands in the army of independence. As early as the year 1776, Dr. Franklin had been sent over to France, in an endeavour to engage the government of that country towards the recognition and support of the revolutionary government. Negociations for this purpose were now carried on with zeal by both parties, and resulted in the conclusion of a treaty of commerce and alliance between the American commissioners and the French government, on the 6th February, 1778.

CHAP. III.

THE AMERICAN REVOLUTION (*continued*).

On the 13th of March, 1778, the Marquis de Noailles, ambassador from the Court of France, presented a note to the English government, formally announcing the treaty which had been lately signed between France and the United States of America. In consequence of this intimation our ambassador, Lord Stormont, was recalled from Paris, and shortly after the Marquis de Noailles from London, and both sides prepared for war. The English people began now to rally loyally round the standard of their sovereign, and private subscriptions were opened for reinforcing the King's army, which were responded to so eagerly, that fifteen thousand men were speedily added to the previous forces of the United Kingdom.

There was now, however, a large and influential party in this country, which desired to see the war put an end to by the recognition of American independence on the part of the British Crown. The Duke of Richmond, as leader of this section of politicians, came down to the House of Lords on the 7th of April in order to move an address to the King, beseeching His Majesty to withdraw his fleets and armies from the thirteen revolted colonies, and to make peace with them on such terms as might secure their good will. The great Lord Chatham, hitherto the ardent friend of America and its liberties, had for some time past expressed himself very strongly against every idea of dissevering the British empire, as he termed it, by recognising the total independence of that country. The great statesman was now very advanced in years, and his bodily infirmities had for some time past greatly increased, nevertheless, when he heard of the Duke of Richmond's intended notion, he resolved, ill as he was, to go down to the House and oppose it. On the appointed day he came in, supported on either side by his son, William Pitt, and by Lord Mahon. "My Lords," he said, in rising to speak, "His Majesty succeeded to an empire as great in extent as its reputation was unsullied. Shall we tarnish the lustre of that empire by an ignominious surrender of its rights? Shall we now fall prostrate before the house of Bourbon? Surely, my Lords, this nation is no longer what it was! Shall a people that, seventeen years ago, was the terror of the world, now stoop so low as to tell its ancient inveterate enemy: 'Take all we have; only give us peace?' It is impossible! I wage war with no man or set of men. I wish for none of their employments, nor would I co-operate with men who still persist in unretracted error. But, in God's name, if it is absolutely necessary to declare either for peace or war, and the former cannot be preserved with honour, why is not the latter commenced without hesitation? I am not, I confess, well informed of the resources of this kingdom, but I trust it has still sufficient, though I know them not, to maintain its just rights. My Lords, any state is better than despair. Let us at least make one effort, and if we must fall, let us fall like men!"

The Duke of Richmond replied in a temperate speech to Lord Chatham. He said: " My Lords, there is not a person present who more sincerely wishes than I do that America should remain dependent on this country. But as I am convinced that it is now totally impracticable, I am anxious to retain the Americans as allies, because if they are not on terms of friendship with us they must necessarily throw themselves into the arms of France; and if we go to war with France, on account of her late treaty, the colonies will look upon themselves as bound in honour to assist her." He then alluded in affectionate terms to the services of Lord Chatham to his country, during the "seven years war," i. e. from 1756—1763. " The name of Chatham," he continued, " will ever be dear to Englishmen; but while I grant this, I am convinced that the name of Chatham is not able to perform impossibilities; and that even high and respectable as it is, the present state of the country is by no means what it was when the noble earl was called to direct our councils. We had then America for us; we have now America against us; instead of Great Britain and America against France and Spain, it will now be France, Spain, and America against Great Britain."

The Earl of Chatham rose up to reply; but overcome with excitement and exhaustion sank back into the arms of his friends; he had in fact experienced a paralytic seizure. The House immediately adjourned in confusion, and the great statesman was conveyed back to his seat at Hayes, where he expired on the 11th of May. A public funeral was accorded to his remains, and as a mark of gratitude for his great services, his debts were paid by the nation.

But it is time to return to the seat of war. The news of the treaty with France met with an enthusiastic reception in America, where a day was set apart for public thanksgiving to Heaven for the grant of so great a boon as it was regarded. During the early spring of this year Lord North, the Prime Minister, had proposed and carried through the British Parliament two bills, the object of which was to bring about a final reconciliation with America, by granting her every possible privilege short of absolute independence of the mother country. Certain commissioners were appointed to negociate terms with the American leaders, and arrived for that purpose on the American coast in the month of May, 1778. Had measures of this description been pursued by the English Government six months before, they might have met with a very different reception; as it was, however, the Congress flushed with their military successes and the recent treaty with France, refused to confer with the commissioners at all, unless on the basis of a recognition of their entire independence. The war therefore continued, but in a very languid state as far as the principal forces were concerned, although Count d'Estaing arrived on the American coast during the course of the summer, with a fine fleet and army under his command. At the same time, however, some atrocious occurrences took place in the back settlements, in consequence of the employment of savages in this unnatural war. The beautiful village of Wyoming on the banks of the Susquehanna river was attacked by a party of Tories, or adherents to the King, and Red Indians, and completely destroyed under circumstances of the most shocking barbarity.* Several other atrocities of a similar nature took place before the close of the war, well justifying the indignant eloquence which had burst from the lips of Lord

---

* This sad occurrence has been made familiar to many minds by the genius of the poet Campbell in "Gertrude of Wyoming."

Chatham, on hearing of the employment of the savage tribes by the English government.*

In the course of the year 1779, the Spanish Government declared war against us, and allied themselves with America and France, their great object being to recover the important fortress of Gibraltar, which had been so long in British hands. In 1780 the States-General of Holland were brought openly to avow a treaty which they had concluded with America some time previously, and war was declared against them by the British government. Thus England had at this time one of the most formidable confederacies both by sea and by land to tax her powers of resistance. The northern powers of Europe, surrounding the Baltic Sea, at the same time formed themselves into a kind of league, which they called an armed neutrality, the principal object of which, however, was resistance to the British claim of the right of searching neutral ships, and of confiscating any articles found in them which our government might consider as "contraband of war." † At this period England had scarcely a single ally in the civilised world!

The hitherto languid course of the war in North

---

* Speech in House of Lords, 20th November, 1777.

† This term was applied to arms and ammunition of every kind, and also forage, which was being conveyed under a neutral flag to any beleaguered fortress. The great powers of Europe and America are by no means yet agreed on all points as to what are to be considered articles contraband of war, and what are not.

America was somewhat enlivened towards the close of the year 1780 by a remarkable circumstance. General Benedict Arnold had been up to that period, one of the most zealous and efficient commanders in the army of the United States. About that time, however, he married a lady of a family loyal to the Crown, and this circumstance together with some disgrace which he had fallen into with the commander-in-chief, General Washington, seems to have disposed his mind to the idea of deserting the cause of his countrymen, and embracing that of the King of England. He entered accordingly into a correspondence with Sir Henry Clinton and his Adjutant-General, Major André, making use of a feigned name; but giving such broad hints on several important points, as left those officers little or no doubt, who was their correspondent. For this purpose he demanded an interview with Major André, which was granted, and André was conveyed by Arnold's directions to the American territory. On his attempting to return, however, he was seized, and his papers having been searched, the treachery of Arnold was exposed. This latter officer contrived to escape to the British lines, but the unfortunate Major André was tried by a council of war, and condemned to be hung as a spy, which sentence was carried out in the month of October, 1780.

During the year 1781 the war continued as before to languish until towards the autumn, when Washington, in concurrence with the French general and admiral, determined to strike some decisive blow. Lord Cornwallis was at that time commanding a detachment of the British army consisting of about 7000 men * at York in Virginia. This place was situated near the confluence of the rivers York and James; it was described some time before by Cornwallis himself as of little value for a military station. To this place Washington and Count Rochambeau determined to lay siege with a force greatly superior to that of the English general. The latter when he began to see the perils of his position, shut in as he was both by land and sea, contrived to send a despatch to Sir Henry Clinton imploring that officer to make every effort in order to rescue himself and his army from the disgrace of a surrender. In the meantime, the besieging army began to throw in shells upon the town and the adjoining British fleet, one of the vessels of which blew up in consequence. Sir Henry Clinton on receiving Lord Cornwallis's despatch, seems to have exerted himself as became him in order to relieve the Virginian forces. His fleet, however, was so dilatory in its movements, that the force which he despatched only reached York River in order to hear the sad news of the capitulation of the British army in York. Lord Cornwallis had been reduced at length by the dreadful

* A great part of these were quite disabled from an epidemic disease, which had spread among them.

E

condition of his troops to come to terms with Washington, in consequence of which he and his men marched out of the town on the 19th of October, laying down their arms in presence of the French and American armies; and with this disastrous occurrence the war was practically brought to a close.

Public opinion had by this time undergone a great change in England with reference to the American contest, the disasters which had befallen our army at Saratoga and York Town contributing not a little to that result. Lord North's government had become very unpopular; so much so, indeed, that on the 20th of March, 1782, that nobleman felt it his duty to place his resignation of office in the King's hands. He was succeeded by Lords Rockingham and Shelburne and Mr. Fox, all of whom were of the party which had from the first strived to bring about a reconciliation with America. On this point all parties had by this time become agreed, the principal dispute now being whether the recognition of American independence should precede or follow the conclusion of a treaty of peace with that country. Commissioners were sent over to Paris to confer with Dr. Franklin and several other gentlemen who were associated with him for that purpose. Negociations for peace were about the same time opened with France and Spain.

During the month of May news arrived in Europe of a splendid naval victory gained by the English

Admiral Rodney over the French fleet under the Comte de Grasse. The engagement took place in the West Indian seas, the French fleet having sailed thither in order to attack the island of Jamaica and wrest it from the English sway. This exhilarating intelligence did not, however, turn away the minds of the British cabinet from their primary object — the conclusion of peace — and the negociations for this purpose went on without interruption. Dr. Franklin proposed the cession of Canada to the United States, a proposition which he was not long in finding to be utterly inadmissible on the part of the English government. There were two other principal subjects of dispute; firstly, the right of the Americans to enjoy the fisheries off the coast of Newfoundland, and secondly, the claim of the American loyalists to indemnification for the loss of property, &c, during the war. The latter point was not urged in the end by the English ministers; and with regard to the former, the American claims were conceded, an equivalent being given to this country in the right to navigate the Mississippi river. On these terms, then, the preliminaries of peace were signed between the two countries at Paris on the 30th November, 1782, while those with France and Spain were not concluded until the 10th of January of the following year, the Spanish government insisting for a long time on the fortress of Gibraltar being ceded to them, a point which they were finally, however, induced to abandon. The definitive treaties of peace were not concluded until the 3rd of September, 1783. From that day the history of the United States ceases to have any closer connection with our own (unless, indeed, that of kindred, language, and religion) than that of other countries of the civilised world. The words used by George the Third on announcing the conclusion of peace with America, will worthily conclude the present section. " In thus admitting their separation from the Crown of these kingdoms," said his Majesty, " I have sacrificed every consideration of my own to the wishes and opinions of my people. I make it my humble and earnest prayer to Almighty God that Great Britain may not feel the evils which might result from so great a dismemberment of the empire; and that America may be free from the calamities which have formerly proved in the mother country how essential monarchy is to the enjoyment of constitutional liberty. Religion, language, interest, affections may, and I hope will, yet prove a bond of permanent union between the two countries. To this end neither attention nor disposition on my part shall be wanting."

SECTION II.

BRITISH NORTH AMERICA. — PART II.

CHAPTER I.

HISTORY OF CANADA.

ALTHOUGH deprived of an enormous territory by the revolt of the thirteen North American colonies in 1776, Great Britain still holds under her sway on that continent, vast possessions, comprising in their extent an area of some 4,000,000 square miles, possessing immense capabilities in the way of inland navigation, and with a great variety of resources, animal, vegetable, and mineral.

Of this vast region, but a very small portion has, up to the present time, probably ever been trodden by the foot of man. The British settlements comprise a small portion of the coast, with some important islands on the east and west sides of the continent in its northern extremity; the inland territory has a small sprinkling of aboriginal inhabitants, who appear for the most part to lead a migratory life over its immense surface of mountain, prairie, lake, and river.

The original discoverer of this portion of America, was John Gaboto, or Cabot, a Venetian, who offered his services to the English King, Henry the Seventh, for the purpose of undertaking an exploring expedition to the regions of the far west. These having been accepted, Cabot sailed from Bristol in May, 1497, with a small fleet of vessels laden with merchandise, for the most part, as it seems to have been confidently expected that his voyage westward would be terminated by Cathay, the ancient name of Japan and China. On the 24th June of that year, however, he discovered the island of Newfoundland, and afterwards sailed a considerable way both north and south, along the coast of the American continent, in his endeavour to discover a N. W. passage to the Pacific Ocean. Cabot took possession of the territory he had discovered, in the name of the Sovereign of England; but no permanent settlement was made at that early period so far north on the American coast.

The expedition of Cabot was followed up by many other adventurers, who in the course of the seventeenth century, embarked in the service of one or other of the European monarchs, as discoverers of new lands, or to promote commerce, or as the founders of colonies. The great colony of Canada was founded by Henry the Fourth of France, about the year 1600 A. D., with the title of La Nouvelle France, and in 1608 its future capital, Quebec, was commenced by Samuel Champlain. Acadia, or Nova Scotia, also became a valuable possession to the crown of France.

Cardinal Richelieu, about the year 1627, planned the erection of a company of one hundred partners, who were to administer the affairs of the newly-created colony in Canada. This scheme was somewhat frustrated by the Calvinist David Kirtch, who, having fled from France to England, in order to escape persecution, persuaded the English government to fit out an armament which he led against his own countrymen in Canada, where he took possession of Quebec a short time after. The value of the province of Canada was not, however, at that time appreciated in this country, and it was restored to France by the treaty of St. Germains, in 1632.

Louis the Fourteenth, under the influence of the great minister Colbert, founded a West India Company, with privileges very similar to those of our own East India Company. These privileges, however, underwent modifications from time to time, whereby they were considerably restricted. It is to be regretted that the English and French, in those ages, carried on a most barbarous policy with regard to each other in North America; the principal native tribes were enlisted in the service of one or other of these two great nations, and the atrocities which are recounted of their border contests, from time to time during the seventeenth and eighteenth centuries, almost exceed credibility.

After several smaller expeditions during the first half of the last century, it was resolved by the British government to make a vigorous attempt towards the conquest of Canada in the year 1759, this being the period of the "seven years war," one of the most glorious contests ever waged by this country. General Amherst was ordered to sail from New York, and after seizing the forts of Ticonderoga and Crown Point, to join General Wolfe, who was to march straight towards Quebec. A third expedition was ordered to take Fort Niagara, and afterwards Montreal, and then if possible to co-operate with Amherst and Wolfe. These combined expeditions proved ultimately successful, the crowning point of the whole undertaking being the capture of Quebec, after the celebrated battle of the 13th September on the plains of Abraham, where the victory was dearly bought by the loss of the gallant General Wolfe, who died on the field. The French general, Marquis de Montcalm also died from wounds received on the field of battle, and the city of Quebec capitulated on 17th September, 1759. In the course of the ensuing year the whole of Canada surrendered quietly to the English rule, and it was ceded to Great Britain by the French government at the Treaty of Paris in 1763.

Shortly after the conclusion of peace between

France and England, the difficulties of the latter country with her North American colonies commenced. It is a striking circumstance, however, that Canada although originally a foreign dependency, and one so recently conquered by England, remained firm in her allegiance to that country during the war of independence, which in its ultimate results severed from the mother country all the most important colonies of British origin on the North American continent. The inhabitants of the United States during the war of independence, sent expeditions over the Canadian frontier to stir up the people of that province to revolt against the English government. On all these occasions the expeditions in question were completely unsuccessful, the American heroes generally returning much the worse for wear to their own country, after having met with a decided repulse on the part of the Canadians. In truth this latter people were perfectly sensible that they enjoyed a much greater measure of freedom, civil and religious, under the rule of England, than they had previously done under that of France, and in the words of a distinguished writer, " previous history affords no example of such forbearance and generosity, on the part of the conquerors towards the conquered, forming such a new era in civilised warfare, that an admiring world admitted the claim of Great Britain to the glory of conquering a people, less from views of ambition and the security of her other colonies, than from the hope of improving their situation, and endowing them with the privileges of freemen."*

In the first instance the civil law of England was introduced into Canada, but General Murray, the first English governor, having protested against this policy, a bill was passed through Parliament in 1774, by which the ancient Coutume de Paris, the legal system which had formerly been in use in the colony was restored to it, and a legislative council established for the regulation of all matters except taxation.

After the American war, a great many persons who still held royalist views crossed the frontier of the United States, and settled in Upper Canada; an emigration which the British government did their best to encourage by liberal grants of land to the new settlers.

In the years 1790-91, a new constitution was granted to the colony under the auspices of the great statesmen W. Pitt and C. J. Fox. By this act a colonial legislature of two houses was established in each of the divisions called Upper and Lower Canada, the upper house or legislative council being appointed by the King for life, while the lower or representative assembly was composed (in the first

* "Political Annals of Canada." See also the Address of M. Papineau, at Montreal, in July, 1820. M. Martin, part ii. p. 24.

instance) of fifteen members, elected by the 40s. freeholders of the province.

In the year 1811 a second war broke out between the United States and Great Britain. On this occasion the statesmen of the former country seemed to have laboured again under a singular impression, that the people of Canada were willing to revolt against their governors, and only waited for a favourable opportunity to do so, and to unite themselves with the great western republic. In accordance with these views military expeditions were sent both to Upper and Lower Canada in the year 1813. The inhabitants of the colony remained staunch in their allegiance to the British crown, a formidable body of militia were enrolled, and the expeditions from the States proved entirely unsuccessful in their ultimate result. Peace was again concluded between the two countries in the year 1815.

By the act of 1791 the province of Canada had been divided into two districts, termed Canada East or Lower Canada, and Upper Canada or Canada West. This step was taken by Mr. Pitt in order to prevent any jealousies from arising between these two divisions of the country, whose interests in some important respects jarred with one another. The lower province contained the descendants of the old French settlers, who, as has been already remarked, displayed their gratitude to the British government for the benefits it had bestowed upon them by their uncompromising loyalty when the province was menaced from without; but who, nevertheless, retained a good many old customs and traditions, to which their English rulers and the settlers, who had poured in freely among them from this country since the conquest, found it difficult at times to accommodate themselves. The inhabitants of Upper Canada, on the other hand, were mostly either colonists from Great Britain or those royalists who had sought a home there at the period of the American revolution. The French inhabitants of the lower province had, so early as 1778, addressed a memorial to the Crown expressing their apprehensions lest they should ultimately be swamped by the rapid extension of the rival race, and of the Protestant interest in Canada. It appears to have been, therefore, with a view to conciliate the French Canadians, and remove all apprehensions of unpleasant results, that this important measure was resolved upon.

The division of the colony led, in the course of time, to the formation in Upper Canada of the "Family Compact Party," which has been described by Lord Durham as a body of men united together, not so much by ties of relationship as by those of race, religion, and political principles. They were, in truth, either natives of the colony or royalist emigrants from the United States; "the principal members," writes his Lordship, "belong to the Church of England, and the maintenance of the claims of that Church has always been one of its (i. e., the party's) distinguishing characteristics. This party for a course of years almost monopolised the bench, the magistracy, the higher offices of the Church, and a great part of the legal profession; they managed to acquire, by grant or purchase, nearly the whole of the waste lands of the province; they had the chartered banks of the colony under their influence; and, in short, shared among themselves almost exclusively all offices of trust and profit."

The pretensions of such a faction as has been described, from the pen of a governor-general of Canada, of course met with vehement opposition from the first among all men of liberal principles in both parts of Canada; and this opposition ever grew more vigorous in its tone as the colony increased in wealth, enlightenment, and general importance. During the ten years of George the Fourth's reign, several unpleasant collisions took place between the assembly and Lord Dalhousie, the governor, on the right of the former to have the entire command over the revenue of the colony. At length, in answer to a petition signed by about 87,000 inhabitants of Canada, urging a redress of grievances, a select committee of the House of Commons inquired into the matter, and finally resolved that the complaints of the colonists were well founded and deserved redress.

In 1830, the year of William the Fourth's accession,

Lord Aylmer was sent out to Canada as governor. The disputes on the subject of the disposal of revenue became more and more warm; and another subject on which the popular party now laid great stress was that the upper or legislative council should no longer be nominated by the Crown, but elected from the 20*l.* freeholders in towns and the 10*l.* freeholders in the country. In 1835 Lord Gorford was sent out to succeed Lord Aylmer, being accompanied by Sir C. E. Grey and Sir G. Gipps as royal commissioners to examine into the alleged grievances of the colonists.

Lord Glenelg was at that time Colonial Secretary in London; and his Lordship, writing to Sir Francis Head, Lieutenant-Governor of Upper Canada in 1835, speaks thus reasonably: "Parliamentary legislation on any subject of exclusively internal concern in any British colony, possessing a representative assembly is, as a general rule, unconstitutional. It is a right of which the exercise is reserved for extreme cases in which necessity at once creates and justifies the exception." His Lordship added, however, that the King was most obnoxious to the proposed change of the upper house into an elective chamber; and no sooner was the intelligence of this fact received in Canada, than the previous discontents of that colony began to show symptoms of breaking out into a flame. M. Papineau was at that time the head of the French faction, and indeed of the liberal opposition generally in Lower Canada; and he with his supporters, in the two chambers, refused to grant more than half a year's supply to the government of that province, and that with severe conditions tied to it. The majority of the upper house were, however, leagued in support of the government, and as most of the bills passed through the representative assembly this session were thrown out by the council, the two houses were placed in a state of perilous opposition to one another.

In the earlier part of the year 1837 died William the Fourth, after having gained the affections of the British people during the seven years of his reign, by unaffected benevolence in his actions and manners. As it was considered most fitting that the accession of the youthful Queen Victoria should be signalised only by measures of the mildest nature, the money for the payment of the civil expenses of Canada was advanced out of the British exchequer, to be replaced from a sum of 142,000*l.* which was locked up in the colonial money box.

Lord Gorford, the Governor-General, convened the Canadian legislature on the 16th August, 1837; but the vast majority of the popular representatives were hostile to the government and its proposals. This was not all, however, the two hostile parties abused one another through the medium of the press, and the malcontents at length publicly declared that "the wicked designs of British authorities have severed all ties of feeling from an unfeeling mother country," and began to take to arms. A riot took place at Montreal between the supporters of government and the "sons of liberty" as the opposition styled themselves, in which an attempt was made to burn the residence of M. Papineau, speaker of the lower chamber. On account of the exaggerated reports which were received by government of the proceedings, warrants were issued for the arrest of M. Papineau and a considerable number of his friends; he and the greater part of the rest, however, contrived to make their escape from the country. The head quarters of the insurgents in Lower Canada were the villages of St. Denis and St. Charles. These were assaulted by small detachments of the royal army under Colonels Gore and and Wetherall, which were in the end entirely successful. A band of " sympathisers" from the United States were moreover repulsed, by the volunteers of Missisqui, the most northern county of Lower Canada; and some desperate bands having been driven out from St. Eustache, and having surrendered in the Grand Brule district, the province of Lower Canada was restored to something like tranquillity.

Upper Canada became likewise a focus of insurrection in the same year 1837. There the "Family Compact Party" had retained its supremacy, one it must be confessed of a most questionable character, as they had usurped those prerogatives which can only in reason be entrusted to an aristocracy of high birth and predominant wealth and influence, while they were no more than for the great part the descendants of the royalist refugees from the United States during the revolution. The reformers in Upper Canada were recruited principally from the more recent emigrants from the United Kingdom; their principal leader and instigator was Mackenzie, who, with his followers, scrupled not to avow their intention of separating West Canada from the great empire under whose shelter it had heretofore so rapidly increased in prosperity.

In 1836 Sir Francis Head was sent out as Lieutenant-Governor of Upper Canada by Lord Glenelg. The new governor entered on his career with a series of very popular acts, calculated to win the hearts of the people, and the result showed that he had not miscalculated; for, on his dissolving the Assembly in May 1837, the new Assembly was found to contain a majority in favour of constitutional government. The lieutenant-governor permitted all the troops of the line to be drafted from West to East Canada, where insurrection had already openly raised its head, and no sooner was this done than Makenzie collected about 600 men on the 4th December, 1837, with the intention of hazarding an attack upon Toronto, the capital of the upper province. Timely intelligence of these proceedings was fortunately brought to Sir Francis Head, who hurried to the Town Hall, where he found a gallant band of heroes determined to fight for the traditionary rights and liberties of their country. This party was joined by Lieutenant-Colonel Allan McNab, with a body of armed volunteers. On the 7th December they all marched against the rebels, who, after a short combat, were glad to seek safety in flight. About 10,000 of the colonial militia had poured in from various parts of the country to the defence of the metropolis, but they were permitted to depart again in peace to their several homes. Lieutenant-Colonel Allan McNab received the honour of knighthood from the Sovereign for his services at this momentous crisis.

The two Canadian provinces had been greatly disturbed for some time past by bodies of men from the United States, who called themselves "sympathisers," and whose object was to carry money, arms, and, if possible, also personal assistance to the insurgents. The government at Washington sent General Scott to the frontier, and issued proclamations in order to put a stop to these proceedings. At length the English authorities, by their earnest entreaties, induced those of the United States to arrest Mackenzie and Van Ranselaer, the principal leaders in the insurrection, and thus terminated the Canadian struggle of 1837.

CHAP. II.

HISTORY OF CANADA FROM THE UNION OF THE TWO PROVINCES.

In the early part of the year 1838 the Earl of Durham, a nobleman, who had distinguished himself in England as a statesman and diplomatist, was sent out to Canada, bearing the titles of " Governor-General of all the provinces of British North America, and High Commissioner for the adjustment of certain important questions depending in the provinces of East and West Canada, respecting the form and future government of the said provinces." The report which he issued afterwards on the subject, dated London, 31st January, 1839, was received with general approbation by all parties at home.

Lord Durham in this report urges that the east and west provinces of Canada should be henceforth merged into one, and that any of the other North American provinces should, with the consent of Canada, be permitted to join itself to the United Canadian legislature. His lordship further recommended that a general executive and supreme court of appeal should be granted for all the North American colonies, and proposed several modifications in the working of the legislative council. The earl was decidedly of opinion that the more wealthy and independent our colonies became, the more they would be disposed to attach themselves to us by the bonds of filial affection and gratitude.

The Earl of Durham met, however, with very great opposition at home, especially in the matter of an ordinance which he had issued on the day of the Queen's coronation, proclaiming a partial amnesty to the political offenders in the late insurrection. This measure was vehemently opposed as illegal by Lord Brougham in the House of Lords, and Lord Durham was so injured both in mind and body by these proceedings, that he died in July, 1840, in England.

The year 1838 was signalised by fresh insurrections in both the east and west provinces of Canada, which were, as before, aided by the invasions of bodies of " sympathisers " from the United States. In the same year, Sir F. Head resigned the government of the upper province to the great regret of many of the inhabitants, and was succeeded by Sir George Arthur. The " sympathisers " were gallantly opposed by the militia and volunteers of Upper Canada, but they continued to make marauding excursions, and, as the government at Washington appeared quite unequal to the task of repressing them, Sir G. Arthur took upon himself to treat with severity those who had been captured. Some were tried by court-martial and hanged, others were transported to our penal colonies, and the American government scarcely interfered in the matter.

In the summer of 1839, Mr. C. P. Thomson was appointed Governor-General of British North America, and Captain-General and Governor-in-Chief in and over the provinces of Lower and Upper Canada, Nova Scotia, New Brunswick, and the island of Prince Edward, and Vice-Admiral of the same. Mr. Thomson set sail on the 30th of August of that year, and on his arrival lost no time in setting to work upon the difficult task committed to his hands. He thought fit to adopt his predecessor's policy with reference to the union of Upper and Lower Canada, and ultimately influenced the Assemblies of the two provinces sufficiently to induce them to consent to a measure based upon three conditions; which were (1.) Equality of representation for each province; (2.) The grant of a civil list to be settled by the Imperial Parliament; and (3.) Equal division of the public debt.

Mr. Thomson, who was created Lord Sydenham, lived to see his efforts in great measure crowned with success, the union of the two provinces being ultimately accomplished. He sank, nevertheless, under the exhaustion consequent on such gigantic efforts, and died in the year 1841, lamented by men of every party and tone of feeling in Canada. In 1843 Sir Charles Metcalfe was appointed Governor-General of Canada, and although much enfeebled by the exertions of a life of thirty-six years spent in promoting the public good in India, this great and benevolent man undertook for some two years the arduous and loathsome task of endeavouring to still the vehement civil strife which still prevailed, rendering abortive all attempts at improvement in this noble colony. One of the most formidable of party questions at that time was, whether the seat of government for the united provinces of Canada should be at Kingston, Upper Canada, or Montreal, Lower Canada, the claims of the former being supported by Sir Allan McNab and the Anti-Gallic party, while those of the latter were brought forward with equal vehemence by the French Canadians. Both parties have since had the sound sense and moderation to place this question in the hands of the sovereign; in consequence of which the claims of both Kingston and Montreal have been set aside, and Ottawa, situated on the border of the two provinces, has been fixed as the metropolis of both; a most happy choice, and one which we trust will greatly promote the future prosperity of Canada.

Two dreadful fires occurred at Quebec during the administration of Sir C. Metcalfe, in which, though few lives were sacrificed, property to an alarming extent was destroyed, and hundreds of people utterly ruined. Subscriptions to the noble amount of 100,000*l.* were collected in the mother country, and 35,000*l.* elsewhere, for the relief of the sufferers from this awful calamity.

Sir C. Metcalfe, created during his stay in Canada Baron Metcalfe, was checked in his career of usefulness by the ravages of disease. He quitted Canada in November, 1845, and soon after died of a cancerous complaint. The Earl of Elgin arrived early in 1847, as his successor in the government of Canada, where his career was such as to merit the applause of statesmen of various political views in the mother country. Lord Elgin's administration was rendered uneasy by the question of indemnity to the sufferers from the recent rebellion in East and West Canada, a question which both in the colony itself and in Great Britain excited much angry discussion and ill-feeling. Bills were passed through the colonial legislatures, in the years 1838–9, granting loans for the purpose of indemnifying all who could be proved to be real sufferers from the late civil strife. The royal assent was ultimately given to an act passed by the United Canadian legislature in 1840, by which 40,000*l.* were set apart for the purpose just specified. This sum was increased in 1847 by a further grant of 3,613*l.* 8*s.* 9*d.* The working of this measure appears to have been not of a very satisfactory character; many received supplies under its provisions who had no just claims whatever, and it has been asserted that some did so who had notoriously been rebels.

Some disgraceful riots took place in Montreal, when Lord Elgin brought the question of indemnities to a close by giving the royal assent to a bill on this subject, which passed through the Canadian legislature in the spring of 1849. Lord Elgin honourably offered his resignation on witnessing the unpopularity of the late measure, but his conduct received a full measure of approval from the home government, and at the sovereign's request he consented to remain in the arduous position he filled. He soon after received testimonies of affection and approval from the majority of the Canadian legislature, and many addresses of a similar tendency were forwarded to him from various parts of the colony.

CHAP. III.

HISTORY OF NOVA SCOTIA, CAPE BRETON ISLAND, THE MAGDALEN ISLANDS, AND SABLE ISLAND.

NOVA SCOTIA is a peninsula lying off the N. E. coast of the American continent, and connected with it by a narrow neck of land. This fine country contains an area of 15,617 square miles, its length being about 300 miles, and its greatest breadth 104.

It has been supposed that Nova Scotia, or Acadia, was first sighted by the Cabots, in which case, as those great mariners were in the service of our sovereign Henry the Seventh, England had some claim to possession, in virtue of priority of conquest, and such an argument has not been without vigorous supporters. The earliest attempt at colonisation, however, of which we have any knowledge, was made in the year 1598 (?) by the Marquis de la Roche, who, by the command of Henry the Fifth of France, took over a number of convicts to settle in the new world. Acadia was the name given by the French to Nova Scotia, New Brunswick, and part of the State of Maine. Several vigorous attempts towards the colonisation of this region were made by the French nation, in the earlier part of the seventeenth century, but the fine settlement of Port Royal (Annapolis), on the west coast of Nova Scotia, was seized in 1614 by the Governor of Virginia, who claimed the whole country for England, in virtue of its discovery by Sebastian Cabot.

In 1621 Sir William Alexander obtained from King James the First, a grant of the country lying east of a line drawn north from the river St. Croix, to the Gulf of St. Lawrence, this country to be called Nova Scotia. Under the provisions of this grant, a number of persons went out as emigrants thither in the following year: finding, however, some remains of the French settlers at Port Royal still inhabiting the land, they turned their steps homeward again. In 1625 the grant to Sir W. Alexander was renewed by Charles the First, while at the same time an order was created, called the Knights Baronets of Nova Scotia, whose numbers originally were not to exceed 150, and who were to aid the foundation of the new colony. They were to receive 16,000 acres of landed property each, and in return each was to fit out six men for the colony, or to pay the sum of 2000 merks. During the wars of the seventeenth century, Nova Scotia was more than once seized from the French by our countrymen, but surrendered to them again on the conclusion of peace. On the breaking out of the great war, known to history as that of the Spanish Succession, in 1702, vigorous efforts were made by the British government for the conquest of this noble colony. In the expeditions which ensued in consequence, the inhabitants of the New England colonies bore a very prominent part; and, in consequence of their efforts, Port Royal surrendered on the 2nd October, 1710, to General Nicholson. Port Royal was henceforth named Annapolis, in honour of Queen Anne, and although no pains were spared by the French Governor of Canada to stir up the native tribes against England, through the influence of the Roman Catholic priests, who had many proselytes among them, the colony remained in our hands, and was ceded to Great Britain by the treaty of Utrecht, in April, 1713. Great difficulty was found, nevertheless, in inducing the French residents of Nova Scotia to surrender their allegiance to the British Crown, and it was not until 1719, that a large proportion submitted, and these only, it is conjectured, on the condition that they should not be called upon to bear arms against their countrymen, the French. For many years subsequent to the conquest of Nova Scotia by British arms, considerable damage was given from time to time to the interests of commerce, and to settlements there, by the ravages of the Indian tribes, who acknowledged as their leader one Baron Custine, the son of a French nobleman by a native woman. These hostile raids were pretty well extinguished, however, by a formidable expedition which the colonists, with the aid of the New Englanders, made in 1724, against the Indian settlement of Norridgewoach, which was destroyed, and the enemy routed with great slaughter.

On the breaking out of the war in 1744 between the two great countries, France made vigorous efforts for the conquest of Nova Scotia from Great Britain. Several maritime expeditions were fitted out on a grand scale, but all of these proved very unfortunate in their results, several being dispersed by stormy weather, while the last of all, under the command of the celebrated Duke d'Anville, was defeated on the 3rd May, 1747, by a British squadron under Admirals Anson and Warren.

After the conclusion of peace in 1748, the idea was formed by the British government of forming a military colony in Nova Scotia in order to dispose satisfactorily of the troops who had been disbanded on the cessation of hostilities. This plan was warmly adopted by the Earl of Halifax, President of the Board of Trade, and under his auspices it resulted in the emigration of several thousand persons, who landed in May, 1749, at the harbour of Chebucto, where they founded the city of Halifax, the present capital of the colony. This settlement was for some years supported by annual grants from the imperial exchequer to a very large amount.

Our colonists in Nova Scotia, as has been stated above, suffered greatly for many years from the incursions of the native tribes, who were too often (it must be feared) instigated to acts of violence and plunder by the French settlers in these countries. On the breaking out of war again in 1755, the English authorities, distrusting the Acadians (i. e. the French settlers in Nova Scotia) took the extraordinary step of assembling them together, and then shipping them to a large amount to New England, New York, and Virginia. The Acadians cried out against this measure as harsh and unjust, and on the conclusion of peace many of them returned to Nova Scotia, where their descendants at present form an important element in the colony.

In the year 1758 a free constitution was conceded to the province, which included a legislative council, and a house of assembly. In 1761 the Indians entered into a treaty with this country under which they agreed to acknowledge King George the Third as the " Great Father," and to cease from hostilities with his subjects. In 1762 the Treaty of Paris was signed between Great Britain and France; and according to its provisions the former country became sole and absolute possessor of the greater part of the North American continent.

In 1784 New Brunswick and Cape Breton Island were separated from the colony of Nova Scotia, but the latter territory was reunited to it in 1819. Great interest was taken in the affairs of the North American provinces by several members of George the Third's family, and the Duke of Kent especially, the father of the present Sovereign, urged several schemes of usefulness for Nova Scotia, among which was the formation of a road between Halifax and Quebec. This important project has since been more than realised in the construction of a railway communication between these two great cities.

A good deal of excitement prevailed in Nova Scotia about the time of the Canadian insurrection of 1838-9, and various complaints were made against the continuance of the old system of government in the former province, which placed a great part of the legislative power in the hands of a few wealthy and powerful families. In 1840 Mr. P. Thomson, Governor-General of Canada, visited Nova Scotia with full powers, as commissioner from the Crown, to inquire into and report upon the state of affairs in that province. This gentleman recommended that the executive and legislative councils of the province should both be reconstructed upon a more liberal basis than was the case formerly, and his advice was adopted by the home government, Lord Falkland, the new governor in 1840, being charged with the carrying out of this measure. Since that time the condition of Nova Scotia has been tranquil and satisfactory on the whole.

The population was estimated in 1848 at 230,000, the descendants of English, Irish, Scotch, French, and Americans who quitted the United States at the period of the war of independence.

The government consists of a lieutenant-governor appointed by the Crown, an executive council of six, and a legislative council of nineteen members likewise so appointed, and a representative assembly of fifty-one members, elected by the possessors of land yielding an income of 40*s.* per annum. The public debt of the province in 1847 amounted to 77,750*l.*, and the expenditure of the same year was 122,221*l.*, of which 34,815*l.* were defrayed by Great Britain, and the remaining 87,406*l.* by the colony.

CAPE BRETON ISLAND.

The fine island of Cape Breton lies to the northeast of the peninsula of Nova Scotia, being separated from it by the narrow channel, called the Gut of Cansa; it is about 100 miles in length, and its extreme breadth is about 80 miles. This island seems to have been for many years a recognised possession of the French, who were sensible of the great value of its noble cod and scale fisheries; nothing else, indeed, could have accounted for the vast outlays which the French government made from time to time in the construction and repair of the fortifications of Louisbourg, their principal station, which lay on the southeast coast of the island.

In the course of the severe conflicts which raged from time to time between England and France during the eighteenth century, this country obtained possession of Cape Breton Island more than once, but on the conclusion of peace ceded it again to its former masters. Towards the middle of the last century the colonial rivalry of these two great nations may be said to have reached its highest pitch at once in their American and Asiatic possessions. On the breaking out of war in 1744, the attention of the New Englanders was directed with great zeal against Cape Breton Island, and an expedition was fitted out chiefly at their expense, which was directed against Louisbourg. The enterprise was rewarded with complete success, for the governor, Duchambon, in a short time capitulated. The imperial government, however, concluded peace in 1749, when Cape Breton was surrendered to France, to the great mortification of those brave colonists who had principally contributed to its conquest. But it was not long before hostilities recommenced, and in 1758 a formidable fleet was sent forth from the British shores to complete the conquest of this important island. This was effected on the 26th of July of the same year, when articles of capitulation were signed, by which Louisbourg and Cape Breton were given into the hands of England. From that time the island has continued uninterruptedly in possession of this country. It was at first annexed to Nova Scotia, but separated again therefrom and made an independent colony after the conclusion of the American war, when several loyalists from the United States settled in it. In 1820 Cape Breton was once more annexed to Nova Scotia, in the representative assembly of which it has six members. Its population is about 50,000; the principal value of the island consisting in its magnificent fisheries.

THE MAGDALEN ISLANDS.

This small group of islands, which lies about eighteen leagues north-west of Cape Breton, is inhabited by a population of some thousand persons, principally descendants of the French Acadians and whose principal occupation is that of fishermen.

SABLE ISLAND.

This barren and inhospitable coast lies about eighty-five miles south of Cape Canro, and is an appendage of the province of Nova Scotia. It has an establishment, formerly maintained at the expense of the colony, but now at that of the imperial government, for the purpose of supplying shelter and provision in cases of shipwreck, but too common on its shores. The length of the island is about thirty miles.

CHAP. IV.

HISTORY OF NEW BRUNSWICK, PRINCE EDWARD ISLAND, NEWFOUNDLAND, THE HUDSON'S BAY TERRITORY, AND BRITISH COLUMBIA.

THE province of New Brunswick is situated on the eastern coast of the North American continent; it is in the form of an irregular square, and contains an area of about 26,000 square miles. Its principal importance is derived from the timber trade, the produce of the noble forests of pine and other trees within its borders.

New Brunswick was held for a long period by France, and formed a part of her great colony of Acadia. The first attempt at its colonisation was made in 1639, but the expedition for this purpose met with sad reverses, and very little was effected towards the accomplishment of this object while it remained subject to the crown of France. This territory was ceded to Great Britain after the conquest of Canada at the treaty of Paris in 1763; and very soon after this event immigrants from England, Scotland, Ireland, and from the other North American colonies began to flow into it. During the war of independence with the United States, the Indians mostly sided with the republican party, and greatly troubled the British settlers in New Brunswick with their ravaging expeditions.

In 1783, after the conclusion of the war, some thousands of the British troops were settled down in New Brunswick, which in the following year (1784) was separated from Nova Scotia, and raised to the rank of an independent colony. General Carleton was the first governor appointed to the new province; he remained in his situation for nearly twenty years, and by his admirable conduct contributed greatly to its future prosperity. New Brunswick possesses, at present, a constitutional government consisting of the lieutenant-governor, who is appointed by the Crown, an executive council of eight members, and a legislative council of seventeen members, both appointed by the Crown, and, lastly, a representative assembly of thirty-nine members. The population of this thriving colony has increased at a very rapid rate since 1783, when it consisted of 11,457; in 1848 it amounted to 208,012, and is at present (1860) in all probability much greater. The public revenue in 1847 amounted to 127,410*l.*; the public debt is about 80,000*l.* The expenditure, of which the civil list forms an important item, amounted in 1848 to 115,353*l.*

Of late years it is matter of regret that the fine

timber or lumber trade carried on by New Brunswick with Great Britain has been somewhat in a depressed condition. The colonists complain that they were injured by the Ashburton Treaty of 1812, between England and the United States, for the settlement of their mutual boundary. By this treaty, it has been asserted, that some of the best timber districts belonging to New Brunswick were surrendered to their powerful neighbours, for which the British colony ought to have received compensation.

PRINCE EDWARD ISLAND.

This fine island lies in the Gulf of St. Lawrence, not far from the west coast of Cape Breton Island, and the north coast of New Brunswick, from which it is separated by Northumberland Strait; it contains an area of some 2,134 square miles. Its physical aspect is that of a gently undulating country, which was originally covered with vast forests of pine, beech, poplar, and other trees; these have been in great measure removed, but the island is still beautifully wooded, the foliage growing down to the very water side.

After its discovery by Europeans, France appears to have been the first nation which claimed possession of Prince Edward, or St. John's Island, as it was styled under the French domination. During the early years of the eighteenth century it was settled by immigrants from Acadia, or New France, and from that time it remained for a course of years a flourishing settlement. In the war of 1745 it was captured by the British colonists of the neighbouring territories, but was restored to France at the conclusion of hostilities. Its final conquest by England took place simultaneously with that of its other present North American colonies during the seven years war (1756–63). At this period the number of French settlers on the island amounted, according to Haliburton, to 4,100, whose principal occupation was agriculture, 1200 bushels of corn being transported thence every year to Quebec. A large proportion of these settlers were condemned to leave the country by its new possessors, some returning to the neighbouring continent, others to their mother country, France.

Various schemes were now proposed for the colonisation of the island. The Earl of Egmont, First Lord of the Admiralty, had the hardihood to put forward a plan of "feudal tenure" after the model of the dark ages of Europe, according to which he himself was to be Lord Paramount of the island, having under him barons, each of whom were to erect a stronghold there to maintain a certain number of men-at-arms, with the right of possession to a certain portion of the land, which they were to hold by feudal tenure from him. This wild scheme was, it is scarcely necessary to add, rejected by the home government, and another adopted in its stead, according to which the island was divided into townships, of about 20,000 acres each, and these were made prizes in a grand lottery, to which a certain description of persons, principally officers of the army and navy, were alone permitted to be subscribers. This enterprise was carried out in the year 1767, and by it the whole island passed into the hands of a few proprietors, with the exception of the land belonging to a few county towns, and a fishing company; its result appears to have been of an unsatisfactory nature.

In 1769 this island was raised to the rank of an independent colony, although there were not at that time more than one hundred and fifty families resident there. In 1770 the first governor, Mr. Paterson, was appointed, and in 1773 this gentleman assembled the first provincial legislature. The war of independence was at this time raging in North America, and in 1775 Charlotte, the principal settlement of Prince Edward island, was invaded by two American cruisers, who plundered it, and carried off the governor and some other authorities of the place. Their conduct was not, however, approved by the American government, which released the prisoners, and restored the property which had been seized.

The Duke of Kent, father of Queen Victoria, who passed several years in North America, paid great attention to the concerns of this colony, which has received its name of Prince Edward Island from the memory of that illustrious personage. The monopoly of land which resulted from the original plan of settlement, to a few privileged individuals, was found to have greatly retarded the progress of the colony, and accordingly efforts have been made from time to time during the present century, to bring this unsatisfactory state of things to a close, by escheating (or depriving of their property) all those (the greater number) who were behind hand with their rent. In 1803 the Earl of Selkirk took over 800 Highlanders to Prince Edward Island, the number of whose descendants now amounts to some thousands.

The present population of Prince Edward Island is estimated at between 60,000 and 70,000; at the beginning of this century it was only 20,000. The colony has a lieutenant-governor, an executive council of nine members, and a legislative council of six members appointed by the Crown; there is also an assembly of twenty-four members elected by popular suffrage. In 1847 the public revenue amounted to 22,631*l.*; the expenditure in the same year amounted to 21,574*l.* The cost of the civil establishment of this, as of other small colonies, has heretofore been defrayed by the Crown and Parliament of Great Britain.

NEWFOUNDLAND.

The Island of Newfoundland, at the entrance of the Gulf of St. Lawrence, comprises an area of some

36,000 square miles, and measures in its extreme length 419 miles, in its width 300 miles. According to the traditions of the Irish and Norwegian people, it is probable that this important territory was not unknown to adventurers of western Europe during the middle ages. It was sighted by Sebastian Cabot in his voyage of discovery in 1497, made under the patronage of Henry the Seventh, and named Newfoundland. It was not long before the attention of all the maritime nations of Europe was directed towards the noble fisheries on the coast of this island, and there is a statement of the crew of an English vessel, which in the early part of the sixteenth century found there some forty vessels, Portuguese, French, and Spanish, engaged in this occupation. In 1583, Sir Humphrey Gilbert undertook the lead of an adventurous expedition to the shores of Newfoundland, which met with a most melancholy fate, scarcely any remnant surviving to tell its sad history.

Several other expeditions of a similar character took place during the reign of Elizabeth, but little appears to have been effected towards the settlement of Newfoundland as an English colony. In the course of the following century a good deal of attention was paid to the subject, and at the middle of that period there were some 350 English families settled on the island. In 1663 an order was issued by the home government to the Lord Treasurer and to certain others, "to erect a common fishery as a nursery for seamen." Later in the century, however, the prosperity of the colony was checked by the wish of a few individuals to monopolise the fisheries of this fine coast.

After the revolution of 1688 war raged fiercely between Great Britain and France, and the French government was charged by that of William the Third with encroaching on the chartered rights of Englishmen to the fisheries of Newfoundland. These charges were renewed at several periods during the last century, when war raged constantly with hollow alternations of peace between the two countries. At the revolt of the United States, Newfoundland and its fisheries received a check, and experienced in consequence a temporary depression. By the treaty of Versailles in 1783, the privilege of fishing on the coasts of Newfoundland was restored to the United States and its citizens, while the islands of Micquelon and St. Pierre, off the southern coast of the same island, were given back to France, with the privilege of fishing in their neighbourhood.

In a few years, war broke out once more between England and France, in consequence of the revolution in the latter country. The long conflict which now ensued between these two great nations, proved, however, beneficial to the rising colony of Newfoundland, and its commerce flourished during a period when competition from foreign countries was most rigorously excluded. At the Treaty of Paris in 1814, Lord Castlereagh signed a document which conceded to the French government the same rights that it had held previous to the great war, a circumstance at which the British colonists in Newfoundland were greatly disconcerted. To add to these troubles, in February, 1816, a dreadful fire almost consumed their principal town and fort, St. John's, and drove some 1500 people, at the most inclement season of the year, to seek refuge amid the shipping in the harbour, or perish in the streets. Another calamity of the same kind occurred in 1847, when the capital was almost entirely destroyed.

The government of Newfoundland is administered by a governor, who is assisted by an executive council of nine members; this body moreover, constitutes the upper house of the legislature. The lower, or house of assembly, is composed of fifteen members, of whom St. John's returns three, Conception Bay four, and the other districts one member each. There is a very liberal elective franchise. In 1785 the population of Newfoundland was computed at 10,224; in 1806 at 26,505; in 1845 the result of the census gave it as 96,687; it is now probably a good deal over 100,000. In 1848 the revenue of the colony amounted to 59,300*l.*, while its expenditure was 62,711*l.*

It is matter of regret, that the interests of our fishermen off the coast of Newfoundland, have been neglected by the British government of late years. It has been mentioned how, during the long war between this country and France, the whole continent of Europe was excluded for years from the British North American fisheries. After the conclusion of peace, however, the French government, by bestowing bounties, contrived to rouse the zeal of their countrymen towards the prosecution of these fisheries; the government of the United States pursued a similar course, and the consequence has been, that of late years our colonists in Newfoundland have complained that its noble fisheries have been entirely removed from their hands, to those of foreigners, to whom, instead of ourselves, these coasts have become "great nurseries" of seamen.

THE HUDSON'S BAY TERRITORY AND BRITISH COLUMBIA.

To the north and west of the cluster of British colonies just described, lies a vast territory amounting to between two and three million square miles, bounded on the north by the Arctic Ocean, while its southern limit was settled some years back by a treaty between Great Britain and the United States, whereby the 49° parallel of north latitude, was defined as the boundary of their respective territories from Lake Superior to the western limits of the continent. This vast region possesses perhaps the finest inland water communication in the world, from its noble rivers and lakes; the land is, however, described as being for the most part barren and rugged, while the climate of a great portion is almost too severe for human existence. The native population of this immense territory is estimated as something less than 100,000, consisting of Esquimaux, who inhabit the shores of the Arctic seas, Indians and half-breeds, or the offspring of Europeans by women of Indian blood. These thinly scattered tribes lead a free and adventurous life, roaming from one portion to another of this vast continent and its adjacent islands.

The first discoverers of the northern limits of the American continent were Sebastian Cabot (1517), Davis (1585), and Hudson (1610), after whom the great inland sea called Hudson's Bay is named. In 1616 Baffin discovered the great bay which bears his name. In the latter part of the seventeenth century the idea was suggested to the celebrated Prince Rupert of forming a mercantile company to trade in Hudson's Bay and its neighbourhood, these regions having been ascertained to possess animals whose furs are of great value. The idea was entered into with alacrity, and in 1670 the celebrated corporation, known by the name of the Hudson's Bay Company, was inaugurated by Prince Rupert, Lord Ashley, and some other influential persons. The limits of its operations were at subsequent periods augmented, until they embraced all the north-eastern portion of the British territory in

America. The charters originally granted by government to the company have been extended in the years 1821 and 1838, when special privileges were granted to it over the Indian territories in those parts of North America beyond the limits of the charter which the Hudson's Bay Company at present enjoy.

These privileges were withdrawn in the year 1858, upon the occasion of a new colony, under the name of British Columbia, being formed on the north-west coast of the continent. This last-mentioned colony comprises the district watered by the Columbia and Fraser rivers between Lat. 49° and 50° (north). Vancouver's Island is, moreover, appended to this newly formed settlement, that island containing about 10,000 Indians, generous, brave, and industrious, but much given to predatory habits.

British Columbia has attracted great notice during the few last years, especially as regards the district of the Fraser river, from the report of gold being had there in superfluity for the mere trouble of digging. There seems little or no doubt of the reality of these representations, which have caused the tide of immigration to set in towards British Columbia of late from every part of the world. How far, though, the human species may ultimately be destined to become profiters from the revulsion in affairs consequent upon the discovery of gold diggings here and elsewhere, will be a problem more easy for futurity than the present time to decide.

SECTION III.

THE WEST INDIES.

CHAPTER I.

DISCOVERY AND COLONISATION BY EUROPEAN NATIONS.

It was on the 12th of October, 1492, that after days and weeks of agonising suspense, land was first hailed by Columbus and his companions on the opposite extremity of the great western ocean. The first place at which they touched was S. Salvador, one of the large group of islands called the Bahamas, and Columbus believing that he had arrived at one of those islands on the coast of Cathay (China) or of India, spoken of by the Venetian traveller Marco Polo, designated the inhabitants whom he found there as "Indians," and the whole region as the "West Indies." In the progress of this (his first expedition westward) Columbus discovered many of the smaller islands of the Bahama and Caribbean groups, as well as the magnificent Cuba and Hayti, of which the wealth was formerly supposed to be inexhaustible.

Columbus was received with great honour on his return to Europe, and set sail again next year for the regions of the west, where he had left a portion of his former companions; these, however, he found on his return entirely destroyed, partly by quarrels among themselves and partly from warfare with the Indians, whom they had injured and insulted. During the second expedition he discovered the Windward Islands, or northern Caribbean group, and on the 2nd of May, 1494, he sighted the beautiful island of Jamaica.

These regions appear to have been inhabited then by two very different races of men. The former of these comprised the natives of the Bahama group, as well as those of the large and beautiful islands of Cuba, Jamaica, Hayti, and Porto Rico. These people were described by their first European visitors as approaching very nearly to the ideal excellence of what has been termed the "Golden Age" of human existence. Their gentleness and pleasant manners, their utter guilelessness and absence from almost all the vices of a more artificial state of civilisation, have been eulogised by the enthusiastic chroniclers of these early expeditions to an extent which may well excite suspicion in every cautious mind as to their accuracy. At the same time the description given of their manner of life may lead us safely to conclude that these islanders were little, if at all, removed from the purely savage state. Their habitations were wigwams constructed of the trunks of trees, they went about almost or entirely naked, and painted their bodies after the fashion of most barbarous nations. Their men are said to have been generally contented with one wife, but allowed their "caciques" or hereditary kings the privilege of having twenty.

The other race of men spoken of inhabited the Caribbean islands, and were denominated by the Spaniards "Caribs." They showed a ferocious disposition from the very first, and made desperate attempts to prevent the landing of their new visitors. They have also had the horrible charge of cannibalism brought against them, though later writers, as Labat, have informed us that they did not commit this atrocity systematically, but only under the influence of angry passions. It will be seen, indeed, in the sequel of this narrative that the conduct of the Spaniards themselves to the unfortunate natives of those regions was but one degree removed from cannibalism itself, so to speak.

Whatever in truth may have been the virtues of either of these nations, and however nearly one of them may have approached the "Golden Age" of existence, one fact is certain, that the happy state of things thus described ceased among them from that day when Columbus first knelt on their shores, and took formal possession of them in the name of the Spanish sovereigns Ferdinand and Isabella. These poor islanders were furthermore not destined to pass through the comparative happiness of a "silver" age, such as we read of in the fables of the older world; they were consigned at once, almost without a tear of compassion from the ranks of their cruel conquerors, to a state of "iron" servitude, which is without a parallel, we believe, in the world's history. They were speedily made to work in those mines, the existence of which they had disclosed in their simplicity to Columbus and his followers, and being a race of slender frame and incapable of any great physical exertion, they began ere long to sink under the fatigue thus induced, or to hide themselves in the woods from their oppressors. For this latter mishap the Spaniards were not without a remedy; they trained bloodhounds to track out the unhappy wretches, a task which the ferocious animals often performed with deadly effect, tearing their victims limb from limb. Nay, we are told that they fed their dogs on the flesh of the natives, it being not unusual to borrow a limb of a human being from a neighbour, this human being having been cloven in two by them in their drunken revels, when they took bets who should perform the atrocity with most success. What name other than cannibalism can we apply to these frantic excesses?

But there was another even more potent cause to induce the rapid diminution and final extinction of the aboriginal race of men in the West Indies. The Europeans committed such excesses of debauchery among the once peaceful villages and houses of the natives, as speedily induced the appearance among them of a disease hitherto unknown in the world, most shocking in its symptoms, and fatal in its effects beyond any other.

The result of these several causes combined may be explained in few words. These regions are described as having been densely peopled at the period of their discovery. The West India islands alone, are estimated to have contained several millions of inhabitants. Hayti contained above a million of people at the period of its discovery, but in fifteen years' time the cruelty of the Spaniards had reduced them to sixty thousand; in forty-three years to five hundred; and shortly after this last period the entire race had disappeared from the earth. The history of the other islands, as far as these unhappy natives were concerned, presents few points of difference from that of Hayti, and all arrive at the same conclusion, the utter destruction, namely, of the aboriginal race of men.

It is painful to record as it is to read this sad episode in human affairs; but history must be candid in depicting these horrors, and the calamities which resulted from them, as a warning to future ages, and a conspicuous evidence of retribution for crime in the natural government of this world. Let it not be supposed, however, that there were no voices raised to condemn these atrocities. From the very first, missionaries had accompanied the voyages of discovery to the west, in the benevolent hope of converting the natives to the Christian faith. Several of these men, among whom the name of Las Casas is the most conspicuous, spent their whole lives subsequently in the endeavour to mitigate and remedy the horrors which they saw around them in America, or in passing over to Europe from time to time to memorialise the government there on the subject, and obtain its interference in behalf of the unhappy victims of the cruelty of their countrymen. Would that we were able to record a successful issue to these benevolent exertions! During one of these voyages of charity, and in order to prevent the utter extinction of the Indians in consequence of the hard labour imposed on them, Las Casas proposed the introduction of negro slaves from the African coast to supply their place; thus the benevolent exhortations of this good man had the effect of greatly stimulating that traffic in negro slaves, which had already however commenced on the western continent.

Our countrymen first began to navigate the West Indian seas in the year 1517. The Spaniards, considering themselves the sole proprietors of these regions both by sea and land, dealt unmercifully with all other Europeans who ventured among them, either on voyages of discovery or for the purposes of traffic. The consequence of these measures was the adoption of a system of piracy among the French and other European nations; expeditions were fitted out stealthily which, under the names of buccaneers, filibusters, and corsairs, continued for long to be the scourge of those seas, and it is well known have by no means ceased even in our own days to disturb those regions. The general history of the West Indies having been brought down to this point, the following chapters will detail the history of the several British colonies now existing, or which have formerly existed in that region. Under this section will be included the British territories of Honduras in Central America and British Guiana in the South American continent. The Bermudas have been generally regarded as a West Indian group of islands, and were always included among the "slave colonies" formerly; they may, therefore, with propriety be placed within this section of the present work.

CHAP. II.

HISTORY OF JAMAICA.

This beautiful island is most happily situated in a central position with regard to the West Indies generally, and somewhat to the south of Cuba and Hayti. The character of its scenery is bold and varied, the lofty tops of the " Blue Mountains " meeting the eye of the traveller long before he approaches its eastern shore, and the interior of the country presenting alternately noble forests, rich pastures, and fruitful meadows. It is abundantly watered by rivers, many of which are perennial; while its harbours, in their convenience of situation and the shelter they afford to vessels of various size and draught, may be considered equal to those of any other island of equal extent in the known world. Its dimensions are 143 miles in length from east to west, while its greatest breadth towards the centre of the island, is from forty to forty-five miles north and south. The climate of Jamaica is varied according to the character of the different parts of the country, but is generally speaking healthy, though mild and somewhat relaxing. " There are few other parts of the globe," says Mr. Martin, " where an African Creole, and European population can, within the same limited space, find climates adapted to sustain the peculiar energies and preserve the healthy condition of each race."*

When Columbus first arrived in sight of Jamaica, on the 3rd of May, 1494, his landing was opposed by the natives, who had, probably, heard even thus early reports of the cruelties practised by the Spaniards in the other islands. The inhabitants of Jamaica are, indeed, described by Columbus himself and other European travellers in glowing terms, as sharing the virtues of the inhabitants of Cuba, and the other leeward islands, and they are further described as living in pleasant villages, with very neatly-built houses, and as provided with various articles of furniture displaying considerable skill in their construction. These villages were, moreover, very numerous, and inhabited by a teeming population.

Jamaica was first regularly colonised in the year 1509, and under the direction of Esquimel, and Don Diego, the son of Columbus, the Indians were soon extensively engaged in the plantation of cotton and the sugar-cane, and in the cultivation of the vine. Having in the previous chapter recorded my opinion regarding the barbarous system pursued towards this unhappy race of men by their conquerors, I will dwell no longer

* Martin's "British Colonies," part xlvi. p. 90.

on the subject, but to mention the circumstance that in sixty years' time, the period of the British conquest, the aboriginal race had ceased to exist on the face of that beautiful region.

Jamaica was early troubled by the incursions of the French filibusters and other piratical adventurers. From various causes, of which this was perhaps the most potent, the colony founded by the Spaniards in this island seems to have progressed very slowly, so that, in the year 1655, it amounted only to 1400 whites, and about the same number of negroes and mulattoes. The African race had been introduced, as before stated, very early into the West Indies, in order to supply the place of the rapidly diminishing Indians. They were found to be a race eminently suited by their bodily constitution to labour both in the mines and on the plantations, and to thrive under the warm climate of those regions. Sir Hans Sloane informs us, " that when he was at Jamaica in 1688, he knew blacks of a hundred and twenty years old, and that a hundred years was very common among such of them as were temperate livers."* It was not, in truth, the influence of natural causes, so much as the cruelty of their European masters, which prevented the African race from multiplying with much greater rapidity in that part of the world.

It was in the year 1655, and under the rule of Lord

* Southey's "History," vol. ii. p. 146.

Protector Cromwell, that Jamaica was reduced effectually by British arms, one or two abortive attempts having been made by our countrymen at former periods. In that year an expedition was fitted out under Admiral Penn and General Venables, which sailed in the first instance to Hispaniola (Hayti), but proved unequal to the task of conquering that island. They therefore re-embarked, and sailed for Jamaica, whither they had arrived before their approach had been heard of by the inhabitants. After rounding Port Royal, the English forces were landed at Passage Fort, the only military defence of the capital. The Spaniards at once retired into the interior, but were not pursued by the English general, and ere many days had passed a capitulation was signed by the Governor Saci, the terms of which were that the Spanish settlers should become subject to England and her laws, or leave the island, surrendering their slaves and properties to the discretion of their conquerors. The greater part of them, including all persons of note and the governor himself, retired to Cuba, leaving their estates in charge of the negro slaves, with promises to return very soon and expel the invaders. The few Spaniards who remained, and a number of the blacks, retired to the inland country or "bush," which, being of a very rugged and intricate nature, rendered all attempts to dislodge them very hazardous. These "Maroons," for such they came to be called, proved for many years a source of of great disquiet to the English settlers in Jamaica, making frequent expeditions for predatory purposes on harmless villages and plantations, where they sometimes committed dreadful barbarities on the peaceful inhabitants. Another source of annoyance from the Maroons was their harbouring among them the runaway slaves of the planters, whose escape was often greatly facilitated by their assistance.

Penn and Venables both returned shortly afterwards to England for reinforcements, leaving a small body of men to hold the island. On arriving in London they were reprimanded and committed to the Tower, while Major Sedgewicke was sent out as commissioner to the island with a store of provisions, of which our troops stood in great need. The result of the expedition appears to have been matter of great disappointment to Cromwell, who was determined, nevertheless, to lay the foundation of a colony in Jamaica, and for this purpose sent out the wives of the soldiers who had gone out in the joint expedition, and gave orders to his son Henry, commanding in Ireland, to send out 3000 emigrants of both sexes thence to the new settlement. Various causes, however,—among which may be enumerated the reluctance of the soldiers to work in the plantations, and the poverty of the exchequer at home, whereby the regular pay of the troops was then from time to time withheld,— contributed greatly to damp the efforts of the Protector. This latter circumstance was very nearly the cause of a mutiny among the forces in Jamaica, which was suppressed, however, by timely and severe measures on the part of the commandant, Colonel D'Oyley. Various regulations were made by Cromwell's government, having for their object the encouragement of trade between Great Britain and Jamaica, and to secure liberty from taxation to the settlers there for a limited number of years. In 1659 the celebrated " Navigation Act" was promulgated, according to the provisions of which no goods were to be imported into, or transported from "the plantations, except in British-built ships wholly owned by British subjects, and navigated by crews three-fourths of which were also British."

The Spaniards made several vigorous efforts to win back the island of Jamaica to their crown, but with very ill success. The Maroons remained, however, as Sedgewicke had predicted, a thorn in the side of the British settlers. The descendants of the first fugitives maintained themselves for a century and a half among the mountain fortresses of the interior, making descents from time to time upon the peaceful inhabitants of the plantations, in the course of which they committed terrible ravages. In order to counteract and punish these predatory expeditions, those savage auxiliaries, the bloodhounds, were largely employed by the English government, packs of them being kept at the public cost for that purpose.

Little or no change took place in the prospects of the colony upon the restoration of Charles the Second. Most of the Protector's measures were confirmed by the new government, and several very valuable privileges granted to the settlers in Jamaica, who were declared to be entitled to all the rights of British citizens. In the year 1664 the first legislative assembly was convened in the island; this body, however, seems to have indulged in frequent and severe altercations with the government at home.

During the reign of Charles the Second, and while D'Oyley was administering the affairs of Jamaica, the system of buccaneering was openly patronised by the English Government, then at war with Spain, in order to save the expense of maintaining a fleet in the West Indies. The most celebrated buccaneer of that period was one Sir Henry Morgan, who is believed to have had 3000 fighting men and thirty vessels under his command. The atrocities recorded of this man and his followers are dreadful, particularly at Panama, which important city was captured by them from the Spaniards in 1670, and utterly destroyed by fire and sword. On their return to Port Royal, laden with the spoils of their victims, these adventurers indulged in the most frantic excesses, expending quickly in debaucheries of every sort the wealth so dearly earned. Morgan himself settled down as a planter after the proclamation of peace with Spain, and ultimately became lieutenant-governor of the island. The population of Jamaica appears to have increased at a much more rapid ratio after its conquest by the English. Thus, almost at the close of the seventeenth century, Governor Beeston reported the number of souls to be 47,365, of whom 40,000 were blacks. It would be well if history could record any amelioration of the condition and prospects of that unhappy race under their new masters; but the accounts received from eye-witnesses, and these very often persons deeply interested in the maintenance of the existing state of things, lead almost in every case to a very opposite conclusion.

On the 7th of June, 1692, the town and harbour of Port Royal were visited by a dreadful earthquake, by which thousands of lives were destroyed, and the town laid in a heap of ruins. The efforts of the inhabitants to repair these damages were some time after set at nought by a hurricane. The French, moreover, being at war with England, determined to take advantage of these multiplied disasters, in order to wrest Jamaica from that power. They landed on the island in 1694, and made some progress there, committing dreadful atrocities on the defenceless colonies; they were ultimately repulsed, however, with considerable loss, and forced to quit its shores.*

---

* Bridge's "Jamaica," vol. i. p. 322.

In the year 1722 a writer*, who had personally opportunities of judging, informs us that " the English subjects in Jamaica are computed at 7000 or 8000, the negroes at 80,000;" he adds, "a disproportion that, together with the severity of their patrons, renders the whole colony unsafe." As instances of the shocking cruelties practised towards slaves we are informed by the same writer of " parties continually sent out by government against them" (the runaway slaves), "who had 5*l.* a head for every one killed, and their ears are a sufficient warrant for the next justice to pay it; if the negro be brought in a prisoner he is tormented and burnt alive." This last circumstance would be quite incredible were it not supported by other and respectable testimonies.

In the year 1722 the Maroons, who had latterly become very formidable, and were conducted by an able chief named Cudjoe, proved such dangerous neighbours as to require the presence of a large military force in the colony to keep them at bay. The British soldiers proved, nevertheless, by no means equal to their antagonists in that peculiar mode of warfare called bush-fighting, to which the interior of the island is so well adapted, and consequently the Assembly enlisted 200 Mosquito Indians in 1787 to assist in their subjugation. By this time both parties were heartily tired of their long struggle, the colonists finding the war ex-

---

* Atkins' " Voyage to the West Indies," p. 245.

penses an ever increasing burthen upon them. Under these circumstances it was not found difficult to come to terms with the Maroons, who laid down their arms and had portions of land assigned to them in various parts of the island, on condition of their not lending any aid in future to the runaway slaves from the plantations. No measures were taken, however, to raise the condition of these savages in a moral and intellectual point of view, as we are informed by a writer * of that period, who condemns such neglect even on the score of its impolicy. In truth, the colonists, both clergy and laity, generally urged at that time in justification of their not taking any steps to bring the negroes to the knowledge of Christianity, that the difficulties attending such a measure were and ever would be insurmountable.†

From time to time the colony was harassed during the long course of years which ensued on the English conquest by insurrections of the negro population more or less wide-spread and formidable. Thus, during the period of one hundred and fifty-four years from 1678 to 1832, no less than twenty-eight formidable insurrections and conspiracies are recorded, giving an average rate of five or six years for the occurrence of these terrible evils. Besides these, moreover, there were continually occurring outbreaks of more or less dangerous character on individual estates and plantations. With

* Long, vol. ii. p. 347. † Ibid. p. 429.

so little security of life and property we cannot be surprised to learn that society itself was in an incoherent state, that recklessness and immorality spread widely among the colonists and planters, bringing in their train the inevitable consequences of insolvency and ruin. These insurrections of the negro population appear to have attained their greatest proportion about the middle of the last century and there can be little question but that this result was produced by the extreme severity of the "Code Noir," or negro code of laws at that period. After describing the severities of this code, which he endeavours, however, to vindicate, Mr. Long informs us that so ignorant were the negroes themselves, the subjects of it, of the penalties they incurred, that they "might as well be condemned on the laws of Japan or Crim Tartary."*

Efforts were made during the course of the last century by various religious communities in Great Britain towards the conversion of the negro population in Jamaica. The earliest of these was that of the Moravians, who sent out several missionaries as early as the year 1754.

Towards the close of the last century missions were founded by the Wesleyans and Baptists in the island. There are various testimonies which go to prove that their ministrations would have been very successful, had they been allowed to proceed in their good purpose

* Long, vol. ii. p. 486.

unfettered by any restrictions of law. Such, however, was the indifference, or rather hostility of the white population to religious instruction, and so great their jealousy of the negroes being raised to a higher state of mental cultivation, that most stringent laws were passed from time to time, the effect of which was almost entirely to hinder the labours of the missionaries in their behalf. These enactments of the provincial assembly brought them several times into violent collision with the imperial government, whose efforts in behalf of the missionaries and their flocks seem to have been generally frustrated by the underhand proceedings of the colonial legislature, which did not dare openly to resist for any length of time the royal decrees on this subject.*

The Maroons had greatly increased in numbers during the half century, or so, which ensued on their dispersion among different settlements in the island, in the year 1737; from 600, which was their number at the former period, they had risen to about 1200 during that long interval. They were considerably excited by the rumours which reached them of the success of the black population in the neighbouring island of Hayti, where they had risen against their French masters in the year 1790, and, after a long struggle, had obtained the recognition of their independence from revolutionary France. Some injudicious measures passed

* See Duncan's "Wesleyan Mission to Jamaica."

at that time by the government tended further to alienate the Maroons, who at last broke out into open insurrection, and, fleeing as before to the backwoods, managed with only 300 fighting men to keep at bay a force of 1500 European troops, together with a large body of the militia. They were ultimately brought to surrender by the judicious conduct of General Walpole, and by a promise being held out to them of having lands allotted them to live on and cultivate. This promise was broken, and the Maroons, to the number of 600 were banished to Nova Scotia, a climate most severe and trying to their constitutional habits of life.* They received religious and other instruction in their new place of residence, however, and were ultimately transferred to the neighbourhood of Sierra Leone, on the coast of Africa, where they are reported to have proved "useful and happy citizens."

In the preceding narrative of the earlier history of Jamaica, ere the discussion of the question of slavery could influence her prospects, the limits of this work have compelled me to omit certain details which might tend to throw light on the subject; but enough, I hope, has been related to lead the reader thoroughly to appreciate the blighting effects of slavery, and its tendency at once to poison the atmosphere of the home circle, and to wither the resources and prosperity of large communities and mighty states.

* Bridges, vol. ii. Appendix, p. 479.

CHAP. III.

JAMAICA.—ABOLITION OF THE SLAVE TRADE.—EMANCIPATION OF THE NEGROES.

Towards the close of the last century the public feeling in England was violently excited in behalf of the negro race in our West Indian colonies and elsewhere, by the eloquent appeals of Wilberforce and his coadjutors, and the revelations made by them of the manifold evils of slavery. This feeling on the part of the British people was by no means seconded by the white colonists of Jamaica and the other West Indian Islands, who urged the dangers which would inevitably result to themselves from negro emancipation, and professed great indignation at any attempt being made by the mother country to interfere in a matter of such essential importance to those colonies. To such a length did this opposition extend in Jamaica that an extreme party there openly broached the idea of separation from England, in order to unite themselves with the great American Republic, where their interests, they argued, would be better protected.

With all this bombast, however, the Assembly at

Kingston considered it best to allay the indignation then abroad in England by passing the "Consolidated Slave Act" in 1792, by the provisions of which many of the cruel burthens which still pressed heavily on the negro race were professed to be lightened; and by providing for their proper maintenance on the part of the proprietors, it was intended to prevent the terrible loss among them from want of food and other causes.

In the year 1807, the slave-carrying trade was finally abolished by an act of the imperial Parliament, an innovation which was highly distasteful to the "West India" i. e. the slave-holding interest in general. The advocates of this party endeavoured to prove that it was this parliamentary interference with their internal affairs, which was tending to their ruin; whereas statistics go rather to make it manifest that ruin, both private and public, was the inevitable accompaniment of such a state of society as our West Indian colonies then, and for a considerable period previously, exhibited. In 1815, Mr. Wilberforce brought into Parliament a bill, requiring the registration of every slave in the British West Indies, in consequence of a suspicion having arisen that negroes were still secretly introduced into the islands. The Jamaica Assembly were compelled to succumb to this measure, which they contrived by various means to render a nullity.

Gradually the minds of the negroes themselves, in

our West Indian colonies, became stirred on the subject of their emancipation from slavery; they were well acquainted with the fact that the government and people of Great Britain had done all in their power to forward their cause, but had been foiled by the intrigues and manœuvres of a small party in the colonies. At length, to such a height did their exasperation arrive, that in the year 1831, an insurrection which at first appeared to be very formidable, broke out in the western extremity of the island, called the county of Cornwall. The alarm of the planters and other white inhabitants was excessive; they expected to witness or even become themselves the victims of cruelties similar to those recorded of the revolt in Hayti some years previous. The conduct of the blacks of Jamaica during the insurrection of 1831-2, ultimately proved them to be by nature mild, gentle, and humane in disposition. A good deal of property was destroyed in the first fever of the movement, but very few lives were taken by the negroes. " Fifty thousand negroes," says Mr. Martin, "were probably more or less concerned in the insurrection, and out of these, perhaps, twenty were accessory to acts of personal violence. When it is considered how many defenceless families of men, women, and children were completely in their power, and that it is the very nature of war to give a free rein to every evil passion, that, moreover, a large part of these negroes were totally devoid of any religious instruction, that they had groaned and writhed under the lash, and been for years subjected to the most degrading and grinding oppression; the wonder is, and ever must be, not the excesses of the few, but the moderation of the many." *

As soon as intelligence of the insurrection had arrived at Spanish Town, the seat of government, Sir Willoughby Cotton, the commander-in-chief, set out with one or two regiments of the line and a body of militia to put it down, having first proclaimed martial law throughout the island. Sir Willoughby very soon saw how matters really stood, and in order to quell the revolt at once, he offered a free pardon to all who should lay down their arms, a few of the leaders excepted. Upon this the blacks seem to have made up their minds very generally to surrender, when the disgraceful conduct of some of the militia officers and planters, who, contrary to the general's proclamation, persisted in bringing some of those who had been actually pardoned to capital punishment, caused a great part of the negroes to hold back, naturally feeling themselves to have been betrayed. When the movement had been finally suppressed, the punishments which were inflicted on the negroes, are described as having been in many cases most barbarous and cruel; the destruction of human life as having been of the most wanton and unrelenting character." Of the white

* M. Martin, part xliv. p. 45.

population probably not twelve persons perished; of the negroes, there is reason to believe at least fifteen hundred must have been sacrificed."*

After the insurrection had been quelled, persecution fell on the Baptist, Moravian, and Wesleyan missionaries, who were accused of having in some mysterious manner fomented the outbreak. Their chapels were burnt down by infuriated mobs, and violence was done to several of their persons. Some of their number returned to England, where the report they gave of the conduct of the planters and their adherents, tended to inflame the public indignation to a very high degree. Fowell Buxton, the enthusiastic upholder of the cause of negro freedom, about that time asserted publicly, "I stake my character on the accuracy of the fact, that negroes have been scourged to the very borders of the grave, uncharged with any crime save that of worshipping their God." †

The question of slavery, and its bearing on the state of our West India colonies, was now one of the most prominent in the public mind at home, and measures were ere long resorted to in order to bring it to a satisfactory issue. In May, 1832, select committees of both Houses of Parliament were appointed to investigate the state of the question. That of the Lower House was supplied with several very able men, and

* M. Martin, part. xliv. p. 45.
† Anti-Slavery Reporter, vol. v. p. 14.

directed its investigations principally to the two following points: First, Whether the slaves, if emancipated, would be likely to maintain themselves, and would be industrious and disposed to acquire property by labour: Second, Whether the dangers of convulsion were greater from freedom withheld than from freedom granted.

The evidence adduced on these two points was of so decided a character, that a bill was introduced during the following session, having for its object the complete and final emancipation of the slaves in our West Indian colonies. It was proposed at first to make a loan of 15,000,000*l.* to the planters, as a compensation for the loss of their "human chattels," and to enable them henceforth to cultivate their estates by hired labour, like the rest of the civilised world. Even this sum was declared, however, to be too small, and it was ultimately swelled into a free gift of 20,000,000*l.* to the "West India Interest," as it was called. At the same time the idea of an immediate abolition of slavery was abandoned, and an intermediate state of six years, called an apprenticeship, was decreed for all slaves in our colonies, duly registered and above the age of six years, from the 1st August, 1834.

The excellent Earl of Mulgrave, after an administration of about a year and a half, which, it has been observed, "forms the turning point in the history of Jamaica," had the pleasing duties to perform before his final departure in the month of March, 1834, of giving the public assent to the Negro Emancipation Bill, and then travelling about the island to announce everywhere to large bodies of slaves, the change which was about to be effected in their condition on the 1st of August of that year. "There were three circumstances," said his lordship afterwards in describing these scenes to an audience at home, "in the statement I made to them which seemed to excite the greatest interest. The first was when I announced to them the utter and immediate extinction of the power of corporal punishment for women. This was always hailed with lively expressions of gratitude from all my auditors of both sexes. The next was, that though they themselves were still for a certain term to be subjected to limited restraint, their young children were at once absolutely free. The third point to which I would allude, was the intelligent manner in which they comprehended, and the gratitude with which they received the promise, that though a certain number of hours were still given to the masters in return for their houses and grounds, which was the footing I found it best to put it on, still they might, by working for wages at other times themselves, advance the period of their perfect freedom."*

The new governor-general was the Marquis of Sligo, to whose task it was allotted to introduce the

---

* Speech at Freemason's Hall, August, 1834.

system of apprentice-labour, in exchange for that of purely slave labour. The joyful epoch of emancipation was heralded in with the most religious enthusiasm by the negro population. On the evening before the 1st August, many churches and chapels were thrown open, and were crowded by the slaves, who fell on their knees as midnight approached, in silent prayers. As twelve o'clock sounded, they sprang to their feet, and the sound of thanksgiving to the Father of mercies was heard on every side. Equal must have been the delight which swelled the bosoms of those ministers of the Gospel, who had gone through insult and persecution in their cause, but were spared to witness the day of their peaceful triumph. Dr. Madden says with reference to this glorious event in our history : " All the sectarian places of worship were thrown open, and thronged to an unprecedented extent; but I regret to say, that for some reasons which to me are unknown, divine service was not performed in the Protestant (i. e. Established) churches in this town (Kingston)." Unfortunately the whole history of the Church of England in Jamaica up to that point is quite of a piece with this circumstance. There is but too much reason to believe that it was the church of a class, and that a very small one, of the entire population.

It may be well here to pause awhile, in order to make one or two remarks upon the thrilling narrative which has just been concluded. The provisions of the Emancipation Bill enacted, that on the 1st August, 1834, all slaves in certain British colonies, namely, the West Indies, the Mauritius, and the Cape of Good Hope, were to be " to all intents and purposes free and discharged of and from all manner of slavery." All children thereafter born, and their offspring, were declared " free from their birth; " and from the above date slavery was " utterly and for ever abolished and declared unlawful throughout the British colonies, plantations, and possessions abroad." All slaves in the colonies duly registered, and of the age of six years, became from the above date " apprenticed labourers, divided into three classes, of which the apprenticeship of the first two, or predial classes (those at work on the plantations), was to cease on the 1st August, 1840, their labour being meanwhile restricted to forty-five hours per week; that of the third, or non-predial class, was to terminate on the 1st August, 1838. Children under six years of age at the time of emancipation might be apprenticed for twenty-one years, if reasonable time were allotted to their education meanwhile.

It very soon became manifest, however, that the new system was not working to the satisfaction of the real friends of negro emancipation, and several well-known advocates of that cause, principally members of the Society of Friends, set out for the West Indies some time after to witness and report upon the state of things there. On their return, they gave so unfavourable an account of the apprenticeship system, which they asserted to be in practice but a modified form of slavery, that the public mind was once more roused, and a select committee of the House of Commons was appointed in 1836 to investigate " the working of the apprenticeship system in the colonies, the condition of the apprentices, and the laws and regulations affecting them which have been passed." When the report of this committee at length was published, the evils observed in the apprenticeship system were classed by them under several heads, of which the most prominent were the want of regulation in the distribution of time for the labour of the apprentices; the withholding of allowances and indulgences formerly universal; and, lastly, the corporal punishment and other cruelties still inflicted on the people of colour, females not excepted. Lord Sligo, the governor, had some time before addressed the Assembly on this very subject, and reprobated their indifference to the cruelties enacted on all sides of them.

Another head of the report bore reference to the state of education among the children of the black population (those which had been declared free, as being under six years of age, on the 1st of August, 1834). Great efforts were made for this purpose by various societies at home, and government was induced to apply to this purpose the funds of the Mico charity, established in 1710 for the redemption of white slaves from Barbary, and which now amounted to 110,000*l*., and was constantly accumulating, there being no longer any Christians in slavery in that part of the world.

The result of these discussions was that in the month of April, 1838, Parliament passed a new act, to remedy the defects in the former one for the abolition of slavery. This measure was introduced by Lord Glenelg, and of course was highly resented by the Jamaica planters, who sent home a very intemperately worded document, protesting against what they termed unconstitutional interference with the internal concerns of the colony. Nevertheless, they so far changed their minds as to resolve ultimately to follow the example of the other colonial legislatures, and pass a bill through their own Assembly, decreeing the termination of the apprenticeship system on the 1st of August, 1838. This measure was accordingly carried without a dissentient voice, and even apparently amid a certain degree of applause.

The day of complete and final emancipation was signalised by acts similar to those which have been recorded of 1st August, 1834, and by a like peaceful and orderly bearing on the part of the enfranchised community. The governor, Sir Lionel Smith, was urged by some fearful persons to provide against violence on the part of the negroes. He thought differently himself, however, and the result justified his sanguine expectations. " I have," he afterwards asserted publicly, with a not unbecoming pride, " not only without employing the militia, but without raising a policeman, or appealing to the support of a single soldier, amply fulfilled my promise. It has been accomplished no doubt by means which they (the West India interest) would utterly despise—the influence of the religious teachers of the people; the moral restraint under which that people consequently exist; and the loyalty to their sovereign, and the confidence in the British government which these very teachers, calumniated as they have been, have sedulously inculcated upon their flocks." *

It is the opinion expressed by those who were most competent to pass a judgment in the matter, that to such an extent had social and public degradation arrived in Jamaica, that the final emancipation of the black population in 1838 alone prevented the utter ruin of the colony, as well as a servile war, similar in its features perhaps to that of Hayti. The system of absenteeism among the planting interest was so universal that almost utter ruin to them was the consequence at this latter period, capital being the great requisite for cultivating their estates by free labour, and capital was scarcely to be found anywhere on the island. The only species of capital they had possessed,

* Parl. Papers, 1839, part i. p. 3.

as has been well remarked, was their slaves, and so deeply mortgaged were nearly all the large estates that, on their receiving from government the value in money of these slaves, the sum thus acquired was swamped in nearly every case in the payment of their accumulated debts. From this and other causes, which shall be hereafter related, this noble colony has certainly suffered a considerable degree of depression for years past. But there is a brighter side to the picture. The prevailing ambition of the negro population since they have become free citizens of this great empire, seems to have been to lay by a sum of money sufficient to buy a small freehold property, which they may cultivate for themselves, and in so many cases have their endeavours been crowned with success, that whereas five and twenty years ago the coloured proprietors of land were very few and scattered, at the present time there are considerably more than *one hundred thousand freeholders,* " working hard, living thriftily, and endeavouring to accumulate real capital, which has not existed for many years in Jamaica, unless indeed slaves can be so termed."

The other circumstance which has contributed to the temporary depression of Jamaica has been the introduction of foreign sugar into the British markets at a low duty, an inevitable result of the free trade policy of this country of late years. But those who are competent to speak from a judgment on the subject, have asserted that coffee, sugar, cotton, or any other article can by proper management be cultivated at a more productive rate by free than slave labour, and consequently that our colonies need not dread competition with the rest of the world.

The state of the prisons and public asylums of Jamaica has occupied public attention a good deal of late years, and an unpleasant feeling was created in the minds of the colonists some time back by parliamentary interference in the matter, an interference which had clearly become very necessary, as the colonial Assembly refused to legislate on the subject themselves.

The population of Jamaica has increased at a slow ratio for many years past. From the census of 1851 it appears that the number of white inhabitants was 15,000, that of the coloured 250,000. Previously to the act of emancipation in 1834, the number of whites was 30,000; that measure has accordingly deprived the island of one half of the white population. A liberal franchise has been adopted in the colony, the consequence of which is that at present fifteen coloured citizens (including three of pure negro blood) sit in the lower House of Assembly, while an eminent gentleman of colour, Mr. Jordon, sits in the upper house as one of her Majesty's Council.

CHAP. IV.

BARBADOES, THE WINDWARD ISLANDS, AND TRINIDAD.

THE valuable island of Barbadoes is situated about seventy or eighty miles to the eastward of the windward group of the Caribbean islands, in 13° 19′ North latitude, and 59° 37′ West longitude. It is about twenty-seven miles long by twelve miles broad, and comprises within that restricted area scenery of a varied though nowhere of a very bold character. The climate is described as dry and healthy, though subject, like all that part of the world, to visitations from the yellow fever.

Barbadoes was discovered by the Portuguese about the year 1518, and received its peculiar name, signifying a long-bearded man, from a kind of fig-tree found there, from the branches of which hangs down a kind of hairy matter. The island was early drained of its native population by the Spaniards, who carried them off to work in the mines of Cuba, and in this deserted state became a prey for the first European power which thought it worth while to make use of it. This was

England, by whose emissaries it was formally taken possession of in the reign of James the First, and in the year 1605. It remained uncolonised, however, for some twenty years from that period, until on the 17th of February, 1625, forty English persons and seven or eight negroes were landed on its shores from a vessel by Sir William Courtruen, a London merchant. This patriotic effort was greatly damped by the irresolute, not to say treacherous conduct of King Charles' government, which granted patents successively to two different noblemen, by which the possession of Barbadoes was conferred on them and their heirs. The legal contests between these noblemen, the Earl of Marlborough, and the Earl of Carlisle, caused the colonists to feel that they held their estates on the island by a very uncertain tenure, and for years hindered the prosperity of the colony. The effect of the civil contests of that period, in the mother country, was not unfelt in this distant possession. Lord Willoughby, of Parham, was sent by Charles the Second, then in exile, to rouse the loyal feelings of the inhabitants of Barbadoes and the neighbouring islands, in which attempt he appears to have met with great success. Lord Protector Cromwell, however, sent an expedition to those parts in order to confirm the rule of the commonwealth, and ultimately Lord Willoughby was induced to capitulate and return to England, part of the troops under his command having deserted to the republican side. The population of the island about that period appears to have amounted to about 2000.

On the restoration of monarchy Lord Willoughby was confirmed by the King in his previous appointment as governor of Barbadoes, where he remained until 1666, when he perished on an expedition to the Caribbean islands. The old vexed points of the right of various noblemen to the possession of the island were once more revived, and caused great trouble to the colonists for another term of years. At length, at the request of some of the inhabitants, Charles the Second was induced to cancel the various patents granted in his father's lifetime, arrangements being made to compensate the claimants according to their respective rights. The King then took the island into his own hands, and established the planters legally in their possessions. At the same time a heavy tax of $4\frac{1}{2}$ per cent. in specie was placed on all the native produce exported from the island, which has only been repealed during the present reign.

In 1675 Barbadoes was overtaken by a great calamity, in the shape of one of those fearful hurricanes which devastate that part of the world at intervals. Shortly after the sufferings of the peaceful part of the community were increased by a slave insurrection, which was put down with very great cruelty towards the unhappy negroes.

Lord Howe's administration commenced in the year

1733, and though only of two years duration, is celebrated from the various excellent qualities of that nobleman's character. A remarkable trait in the history of Barbadoes has been the liberality that colony has displayed towards its governors, whose salaries have been sometimes called "extravagant" by writers in alluding to the subject.

In 1780 another tremendous hurricane occurred, which caused great loss of life and destruction of property to the amount of 1,320,564*l.* sterling. The most liberal subscriptions were opened in all parts of the empire for the relief of the survivors from this awful catastrophe. The city of Dublin alone gave 20,000*l.*, a fact which was borne in mind by the inhabitants of Barbadoes, who more than sixty years afterwards distinguished themselves by the promptness with which they responded to the cry of distress from Ireland, in consequence of the failure of the potato crop.

The struggle for negro emancipation was distinguished by the same characteristics here as in Jamaica. The planters were equally bigoted in their views, and averse to the dissenting ministers having any influence with the black population. In the month of August, 1831, the island was once more devastated by a hurricane, and for its relief, together with that of some neighbouring islands, Parliament voted the sum of 100,000*l.*

The apprenticeship system gave general dissatisfaction in Barbadoes, and the Colonial Assembly was found most ready to vote its termination on the 1st August, 1838.

Since that period Barbadoes has progressed in a most satisfactory manner, notwithstanding the temporary drawback received by the remission of the sugar duties in 1846. The population of the island, which in 1773 amounted to 18,532 whites and 68,548 coloured, making a total of 87,089; at the census of 1851 was 15,824 whites and 120,115 coloured, total 135,939. The condition of the coloured population has been very favourably described by the governor in 1851; that of the white inhabitants is decidedly unfavourable, many of them being in such distress as to be a burden on the resources of the colony. In August 1838, the oppressive 4½ per cent. export duties were entirely abolished in this and the other Caribbean islands.

St. LUCIA.

This island is situated a little north-west of Barbadoes, in 13° 50′ N. lat., 60° 50′ W. long. It is about 27 miles in length and 13½ at its greatest breadth. Among the beautiful Antilles, St. Lucia is distinguished for its varied and exquisite scenery; it is intersected from west to south by a chain of volcanic mountains, of which some are now frequently in a state of eruption; it is also fruitful in mountain streams, lovely valleys, and rich vegetation.

The island is supposed to have obtained its name from its first discoverers, who were Frenchmen, and from their seeing it on the day of the festival of St. Lucia. During the course of the seventeenth century France and England both made several attempts to conquer it for themselves, out of the hand of its original owners the Caribs: all these must have been more or less ineffectual, nevertheless; for so late as the treaty of Utrecht in 1713, it was regarded as a neutral territory by both powers. A few years later, in 1723, rival expeditions under the sanction of the French and English governments, arrived on the shores of St. Lucia, both having the conquest and colonisation of the country in their ulterior view. The respective commanders, Marshal d'Estrées and the Duke of Montagu, wisely and humanely determined, instead of shedding blood, to refer the matter to the arbitration of their home governments. The island remained neutral, however, until the war which broke out between the two countries in 1744; and at the treaty of Aix-la-Chapelle in 1748, it was determined that it should continue so. At the treaty of Paris in 1763, however, it was made over to the French crown with the consent of England, the claims of the native Caribs not appearing to have obtained the least consideration. Under French rule it prospered greatly;

the Caribs retired to the neighbouring island of St. Vincents; negroes were introduced, and in 1772 the population was rated at 15,476 souls.

During the war which broke out in 1778, the rival countries struggled fiercely for this much coveted possession. Admiral Barrington with an English fleet anchored in the cul-de-sac, and was on the point of bringing the French governor and garrison to surrender the island, when Count d'Estaing appeared at the head of a formidable force of the enemy. His attempts to drive away the English were, however, defeated with great loss, and the governor of the island finding himself once more deserted surrendered to the British commander. During the remainder of the war, St. Lucia became the rendezvous of the British squadron in these parts; on the conclusion of peace in 1783, however, after a prolonged negociation, it was once more surrendered to France.

On the breaking out of the French revolution, the effects of the novel doctrines so injudiciously propagated by the mother country, vibrated through every part of her extensive colonial empire. The blacks rose everywhere in those portions of the West Indies which belonged to France, and fearful scenes of bloodshed and desolation succeeded; one half of the inhabitants of St. Lucia are said to have been destroyed.*

* Parl. Papers, July, 1846, p. 85.

At this crisis the island was invaded by Admiral Sir John Jervis (Earl St. Vincent); a severe contest succeeded, and eventually, the inhabitants being assisted by emissaries from France, then at the height of its revolutionary enthusiasm, the British force was compelled to retire precipitately. In 1796, St. Lucia was again invaded by a fleet and force under Sir Ralph Abercrombie, and after a long siege, its principal position fell into British hands. General Moore remained to contend with the bush-fighters of the interior, who surrendered to him in the course of the ensuing year. At the peace of Amiens, St. Lucia was given back into the hands of France, but on the return of hostilities, was again captured by the British forces under Commodore (afterwards Lord) Hood. The French government seems to have placed a very high value on this possession, for it was described in the report of Governor Noguès, to the first consul of France, as capable of being made the capital of the Antilles, the general market of the Windward Islands, and the Gibraltar of the Gulf of Mexico.

The great event of the last half century has been here, as elsewhere in our West Indian colonies, the abolition of slavery, a measure which the report of the lieutenant-governor, Mr. A. W. Torrens, in 1846, "demonstrates to have had the best possible effects." St. Lucia is a Crown colony having no representative assembly, and its officials being all appointed by the home government. The population in 1851 amounted to 24,185.

St. VINCENT.

This island is situated some 22 miles south of St. Lucia in 13° 10' N. lat., and 61° 5' W. long. It is about 18½ miles long and 11 broad. The climate is mild and soft in the lower country, but on some of the heights in the interior the air is much cooler. There are numerous streams rushing down from the mountains, by which the machinery is principally turned. The island is divided into five parishes.

Tradition points to Columbus as having been the original discoverer of St. Vincent in the year 1498. It appears, nevertheless, to have been taken little notice of by Spain or any other European power for long afterwards, its native inhabitants being a warlike Caribbean nation, who knew well how to defend their coast against aggression. During the course of the seventeenth century several attempts were made successively by English and French to settle in the island, and the latter nation was partially successful, though it was recognised as a neutral territory by the two countries so late as the treaty of Aix-la-Chapelle in 1748. War breaking out again, however, St. Vincent was captured by Great Britain, and secured to her by the Treaty of Paris in 1763. At that time there were said to be on the island 800 whites and 3000 slaves, while the original Caribs had almost disappeared. In 1772 a war arose between our settlers and the Caribs about the tracts of land which they occupied; a war which, in its origin and conduct, is said to have reflected dishonour on the national character.* Ample justice seems to have been done at its conclusion to the natives. During the ensuing war St. Vincent was captured by the French without striking a blow, but restored to England by the treaty of Versailles in 1783. In 1794 the revolutionary doctrines of France penetrated among the black and Caribbean populations of this island, and a fierce contest was the result, which was concluded, after two years of hard fighting, by the banishment of some 5000 of the rebels to the island of Rattan in the Bay of Honduras. A terrible eruption of Mount Souffrierer, a volcano in the interior of the island, took place in the year 1812, which caused great damage to life and property; so much so, that Parliament voted 25,000*l.* for the relief of the sufferers.

The population of St. Vincent, which in 1764 was rated at 9518 souls, in 1851 amounted to 30,128. " Since the memorable 1st of August, 1838," says the St. Vincent Almanac for 1851, " the condition of the labouring population has greatly improved; schools and places of worship have increased, and large tracts of

* Coke's West Indies, vol. ii. p. 187.

land have been purchased or leased, upon which villages and hamlets have been erected." The government is conducted by a popular assembly of twelve representatives, a legislative council appointed by the Crown, and the lieutenant-governor. The small islands called the Grenadines, lying to the south of St. Vincent, are attached to its government. They are about nine in number, and contain a population of some 2000, with five villages.

GRENADA.

This is the most southerly, and is considered the most beautiful of the Windward Caribbean group of islands, and is situated in 12° 10′ N. lat., and 61° 25′ W. long. Its greatest length is about 24 miles; its greatest breadth 12 miles.

Grenada was discovered by Columbus in the year 1498; but its native inhabitants received little further molestation until the middle of the seventeenth century, when it was invaded by the French under Du Parquet, Governor of Martinique. This expedition was successful; but the atrocities committed upon the unfortunate Caribs are described to have been of the most wholesale character. From this time the colony languished in the hands of France until the commencement of the last century, when its population was described by the Abbé Raynal as consisting of 251 whites and 525 blacks, cultivating principally sugar and indigo. During the course of the eighteenth century Grenada progressed very much, and in 1762 fell into the hands of England, to whose rule it was confirmed by the Treaty of Paris in the following year. It became a question whether this island was subject by right to the $4\frac{1}{2}$ per cent. duties imposed on Barbadoes, and the case was argued in Westminster Hall; but judgment was given, in 1774, " against the Crown," and the duty was accordingly abolished in Grenada, Dominica, St. Vincent, and Tobago. During the war of the American revolution, Grenada was retaken by the French under the Comte d'Estaing, but was restored to England by the treaty of Versailles.

At the period of the second occupation by England certain intrigues, in which the governor is said to have had an unworthy part, were hatched, in consequence of which full toleration was not accorded to the Catholic, i.e. the French portion of the community. This led to disputes and ill-feeling, by which the wild doctrines then spreading abroad from France, were greatly promoted. The consequence was a sanguinary insurrection on the part of the negro population here as elsewhere in the West Indies, which was only put down after much blood had been shed, and many barbarous penalties inflicted on the convicted culprits. The colony remained long after these events in a very languid state, has since experienced several very serious drawbacks to its progress in the shape of earthquakes, hurricanes, and pestilence. A most extraordinary blight of sugar ants took place in the year 1770, which continued to prove most destructive to the production of sugar until 1780, when they were at length checked by a tremendous hurricane which swept over the land.

Although while slavery was in the ascendant, the black population was treated with unusual mildness in Grenada, yet the abolition of the entire system has not failed there as elsewhere to place trade upon a sounder footing, and to induce more *general* prosperity.

The climate of Grenada is described as one of "Italian softness," and its scenery as most beautiful. Mr. Coleridge has described the view from Government House, situated on a ridge of Hospital Hill as " the Bay of Naples on one side, and a poet's arcadia on the other."* Two of the small group of Grenadine islands, Cariacon and Ronde or Redonda, are attached to Grenada. They are principally used for the growth of cotton. The population of Grenada was in 1787, 26,071; in 1851 it amounted to only 32,671; this is but a small increase certainly compared with many of our other West Indian colonies, and considering the capabilities of the island. In the lieutenant-governor's Report of the 18th of May, 1852, we find the

---

* Coleridge, " Six Months in the West Indies," p. 95.

following statement of her present condition: "That Grenada has considerably recovered during the last few years from her previously prostrate condition there is no doubt; her revenue is if anything increasing; her imports and exports both show a considerable addition; her population is, irrespective of immigration, adding to its numbers."

TOBAGO.

This island lies sixty miles south-east of Grenada, in 11° 9′ N. lat., and 60° 12′ W. long. Its climate is salubrious: from without, its appearance on the northern side is so stern and monotonous as to have gained it the title of the "Melancholy Isle;" but on a nearer approach the prospect is said to be far more pleasing, the scenery being, however, of a very irregular character.

Tobago was discovered by Columbus in the year 1498, and named by him Assumption; its present name of Tobago, or Tobacco, arose from the use of that herb being observed among its inhabitants. The history of the island for a considerable period, is very confused and uncertain. England laid a claim to its possession as early as the sixteenth century, and since that period various contests for supremacy have taken place between our countrymen and the French and Dutch in the West Indies. In 1764, when at length by the Treaty of Paris this island was given over to

England, a lieutenant-governor was sent there, and a regular settlement made for the first time, the only inhabitants at that time being Caribs. The system of slavery was soon introduced into Tobago and led to some prolonged and disastrous insurrections, the principal of which took place in 1770-1. In 1775 the cultivation of the sugar-cane was almost abandoned in consequence of a swarm of ants which destroyed the plant almost entirely; the cultivation of cotton was generally adopted in its stead. In 1781 Tobago was captured by the French, but was retaken by a British force in 1783. It was ceded to the French in 1802, but having been recaptured by Commodore Hood in the following year, was confirmed in the possession of Great Britain by the treaty of 1814.

Here, as elsewhere, we have to record the beneficial results of the abolition of slavery; Sir Andrew Halliday having remarked in 1837 with reference to this island that "certainly here, as has been proved elsewhere, free labour has been more productive than slavery could ever be made,"[*] to make no remark on the great moral benefits which have resulted from the change of system.

The population of Tobago, which in 1727 was rated at about 12,300, in 1851 amounted to some 15,000; that it has not increased at a more rapid ratio, may be

---

[*] Sir A. Halliday's "West Indies," p. 274.

ascribed, in great part, to the destruction of life in the colony while under the hateful influence of slavery. The government consists of a lieutenant-governor, a council, and an assembly elected by the people.

TRINIDAD

Ist he most southerly of all the British West Indies, and is separated from the South American continent by the small Gulf of Pana. Columbus discovered this island in 1498, and bestowed on it the name of the Trinity in consequence of a vow which he had made shortly before, when in distress from want of water. It was a remarkable coincidence, that the first land he saw after this consisted of three mountain summits, which as he approached nearer shore, proved to be joined at the base. The island of Trinidad has been compared in shape to a stretched ox-hide; its beauty and fertility combined were the delight of Columbus, as they have been of all visitors since his time; the climate is described as soft and pure. The Gulf of Pana, between the west coast of Trinidad and the neighbouring continent, is said to form one magnificent harbour of 100 miles in length. The native inhabitants at the period of its discovery, appear to have been partly Caribs, and partly of the more civilised tribes of the Leeward Islands.*

* Thus Bryan Edwards, vol. i. p. 72, and Humboldt.

The Spaniards for a long period made use of Trinidad for obtaining wood and water on their voyages; frequently moreover, carrying away the simple inhabitants in order to make slaves of them; a regular settlement was, however, made on the island in the year 1532. Towards the close of that century, Sir Walter Raleigh invaded the island, and plundered it in revenge for some unwarrantable proceedings of the Spaniards shortly before. He set at liberty many captive natives, among whom were five caciques, linked together by one chain; these poor creatures he found in a state bordering on starvation.

About the beginning of the eighteenth century, in consequence of a treaty between France and Spain, the French Royal Guinea Company undertook to supply the Spanish colonies with 4800 negroes every year for a term of years. Although Trinidad appears to have shared this advantage, the colony continued in a low state of prosperity during the greater part of the last century. A blight of the cacao, the principal crop of the island, occurred in the year 1725, and another in 1740. Some years later, cabals took place among the inhabitants, ending in an outbreak, which was put down eventually, but not until the colony had been reduced to a very low ebb. Towards the close of the century, however, matters began to brighten, a large immigration of French and Irish was encouraged by the Spanish government, which had no objection to any persons settling among them, providing they held the Roman Catholic faith. The French immigrants so greatly preponderated that Trinidad began to assume the aspect of a French, rather than a Spanish colony. The aborigines were now rapidly becoming extinct, and the most unwarrantable measures were frequently resorted to in order to kidnap people of colour thither from other parts of the West Indies.

At length Don J. Chacon, a naval captain and a man of considerable energy, set in hand a vigorous system of government in this little island. In 1797, a British fleet of ten vessels, bearing some 10,000 men appeared off the coast. The governor could rally few of the inhabitants to his side in consequence of the spirit of republicanism, then so generally prevalent, having found its way to this remote settlement. Chacon did all that was in the power of man, but he was compelled to capitulate in the end to the British under Abercrombie.

This general left his aide-de-camp (afterwards Sir J. Picton) in command of the island, an administration which he is said to have exercised with a rod of iron. After Picton, the chief authority in the island was committed to Sir Thomas Hislop. In 1805, the island was thrown into confusion by the unexpected appearance of Nelson with a large fleet, which the inhabitants mistook for a hostile expedition. In 1808, the principal town, Port of Spain, being chiefly built of wood was almost destroyed by fire, a calamity towards the relief of which Parliament at home voted 50,000*l*.

Some disturbances were made at first in consequence of Methodist missionaries settling in the island. The administration of Captain Sir Ralph Wordford, R. N., who was appointed governor in 1813, and quitted the island in 1828, was a very brilliant one, and Trinidad progressed rapidly under his fostering hand. He was succeeded by Sir Lewis Grant, who again was succeeded in 1833 by Sir G. F. Hill. The change from slavery to general freedom was accomplished without any disturbance.

The population of Trinidad has increased wonderfully since 1783, when it was estimated at 2763, a mixture of Europeans, Indians, free coloured, and negro slaves; in 1851 it amounted to 68,000 persons, of whom 1494 were whites. Trinidad is a Crown colony, and is ruled by a governor, an excutive council of three, and a legislative council of thirteen individuals; all these officers being appointed by the sovereign.

CHAP. V.

THE LEEWARD ISLANDS.

ANTIGUA

Is situated in the 17th degree N. lat., and 61st W. long., being some forty miles north of Guadaloupe; it is fifty-four miles in circumference. Its shores are indented with creeks, coves, and bays, beyond which are numerous rocks and shoals, so that it is a difficult and dangerous coast to approach on every side except the north-west. The scenery of the interior is described as resembling homely landscapes in England, the great drawback of the country being the want of fresh water, which is in some measure counteracted by the system of preserving rain-water in cisterns.

Columbus sighted Antigua in 1493, and named the island after a church in Seville, S. Maria la Antigua: it is not certain whether it had any inhabitants at that time or not. In 1632 Antigua was formally taken possession of by a certain Sir Thomas Warner, with some families of English settlers in his train.

This little colony continued to flourish until the year 1666, when it was invaded by the French from Martinique, and plundered. In the same year, however, it was confirmed in the possession of Great Britain by the treaty of Breda.

Some years afterwards the cultivation of the sugar cane was introduced into Antigua by an enterprising man named Colonel Codrington, who, with the title of Captain-General of the British Leeward Caribbee Islands, held supreme power in those parts for a term of years, and under whose fostering care our West Indian possessions appear to have thriven greatly.* In 1706, on the other hand, the prosperity of the colony received a check from the appointment, by the Duke of Marlborough, to the chief command of a man named Park, who appears to have been in every way unfitted for the important duties he undertook. The consequence of his mal-administration was an insurrection, in which the unhappy man was actually torn limb from limb by a mob of desperadoes. After an investigation into this matter, a general pardon was issued by the Crown to all parties concerned. In the year 1737 a desperate plot was disclosed, on the part of the negro slaves, to massacre all the white inhabitants. The punishments inflicted in consequence were, it is to be regretted, of a very bar-

---

* Schomburgh's "Hist. of Barbadoes," p. 295.

barous character, utterly unworthy of a great civilised nation.

During the course of the last century the influences of religion and morality so far penetrated among the inhabitants of this colony as to mitigate considerably the evils of slavery. Religious and other instruction did more, we are informed, than the dread of torture had formerly effected to prevent insurrection. The entire emancipation of the negroes was effected in Antigua at once, without going through the apprenticeship system. This was a great cause of congratulation to the opponents of slavery, and removed apprehension from the minds of men with reference to the consequences of too sudden a change from slavery to freedom.

The population of Antigua, about the commencement of the last century (1707), consisted of 2892 whites and the same number of negroes. In 1724 it had risen to 25,000 of both races. At the census of 1851 the total was rated at 37,163. "Here, as in other islands, the material condition of the emancipated race is most satisfactory. They are abundantly supplied with all the necessaries, and many of the comforts of life."*

The governor-in-chief of the Leeward group resides in Antigua. There is also a legislative council ap-

---

* Blue Book for 1846.

pointed by the Crown, and a representative assembly elected by the people.

BARBUDA

Is situated some thirty miles north of Antigua. It is nineteen miles in length, ten in breadth, and is for the most part low and flat, resting on a basis of coral reefs. The island was early occupied by a body of Englishmen under a certain Sir Thomas Warner. These were, however, expelled by a Caribbean invasion, but returned some time after and established English dominion there effectually. Barbuda has been granted by the Crown since the year 1684 to a family of the name of Codrington, who hold it on the singular condition of presenting a fat sheep to the governor-in-chief of the Leeward Islands whenever he thinks proper to visit it. There is a great want of fresh water felt here as in Antigua. The present population of the island is very small, amounting in 1851 to only 629 souls.

DOMINICA.

This important island lies midway between those of Martinique and Guadaloupe. It is in length twenty-eight miles, in breadth fourteen. It is quite a highland country, its mountains being of an abrupt and lofty character, and frequently covered to the very tops with the most luxuriant verdure. There is a great want of water, which has been chiefly supplied by a freshwater lake situated on the summit of a mountain, somewhere in the centre of the island. Dominica is divided into ten parishes.

The island was discovered by Columbus, and received its name from him in consequence of his first beholding it on Sunday, 3rd November, 1493. The primitive inhabitants were Caribs, who received an augmentation about the beginning of the seventeenth century from some French settlers; and these latter mixed on very friendly terms with the natives. As Dominica subsequently became the subject of jealous rivalry between England, France and Holland, it was declared a neutral territory, to which all Europeans might resort for the purposes of trade and commerce. Such it remained accordingly until the year 1759, when England and France being at war, and the governor of the island espousing the cause of the latter power, a British force attacked and captured it. By the treaty of Paris in 1763 it was formally ceded to this country by France.

Under the new regime Dominica prospered rapidly, the inhabitants of the island reconciling themselves easily to their new yoke. On the breaking out of the American revolution, however, this prosperity received a check. France having espoused the cause of the American colonists, and made war upon England in consequence, an expedition was sent out under the Marquis de Bouille, in the year 1778, to regain the island of Dominica for the French Crown. This was easily effected through the treachery of some of the French inhabitants, who made our soldiers useless by intoxication. The new French governor, Marquis Duchilleau, behaved so unjustly, and broke so unscrupulously through the articles agreed upon by the military commander with the English settlers, that many of these quitted the island in disgust.*

On Easter Sunday, in 1781, the capital of the island, Roseau, was set on fire by the French soldiers, a deed in which the governor, Duchilleau, is strongly suspected of having been implicated. By this and other unworthy proceedings the prosperity of the country received a severe check. It was restored to England, however, by the Treaty of Versailles in 1783.

In the year 1795 an attempt was made by Citoyen Victor Hugues to rouse the French inhabitants of Dominica to revolutionary enthusiasm, and to shake off the yoke of England. This endeavour was foiled by the gallantry of the militia, and the devotedness of the negro population to the British cause.

A terrible mutiny broke out on the 9th April, 1802, amongst the 8th West India Regiment (negroes) stationed at Prince Rupert's. These men, rendered desperate by some scandalous reports artfully insinuated among them, rose at once and murdered all their officers, with only two exceptions. Johnstone, the

* Atwood's " Hist. of Dominica," pp. 140, 155.

governor, took vigorous measures to repress this desperate outbreak, but the unfortunate men did not surrender until terrible slaughter had been committed among them.

In the year 1805 an incursion was made by a French force into Dominica; great damage was wrought, and a heavy plunder carried away on their retreat.

In 1813-14 Dominica was troubled by a Maroon insurrection, consisting chiefly of desperate people of colour, who had fled away to the mountains of the interior. They were in the end subjugated, but very barbarous measures were resorted to in order to punish them; so much so as to call down the censure of the Imperial Parliament. The last event of any importance in the history of Dominica is the change from slavery to perfect freedom between the years 1834-38.

The population of Dominica amounted in 1768 to 8090 souls; according to the census of 1844 it was 22,000. In 1839 a public meeting of the planters was held, at which " an acknowledgment was made *with feelings of unmixed gratification* of the peaceable and quiet disposition evinced by the labourers as one body since their entire emancipation." Here, as elsewhere in our colonies, they have purchased land largely.

MONTSERRAT

Is a small island about thirty miles south-west of Antigua, estimated to be nine miles long and as many broad. It is very mountainous, and has very few secure landing places from the sea. Of the whole island only about one third part is considered capable of cultivation.

Montserrat was discovered by Columbus in 1493, and named after a mountain in Spain. The records of its history since that period are very few and unsatisfactory. In 1632 a number of Irish Roman Catholics came over from St. Kitt's and settled there. According to Raynal, the new colonists were not content until they had entirely expelled the original inhabitants of the country. The colony flourished after this for a certain term of years. In 1712 a French armament invaded the island, which is said to have been much injured by its depredations. In 1782 Montserrat was captured by France, but was restored to Great Britain at the close of the war. From that period it has remained a British possession.

The population of Montserrat, which in 1787, was estimated at 5115, in 1851 amounted to 7053. The government consists of a president, acting under the governor-in-chief of the Leeward Islands, an assembly of twelve members, and a council (executive and legislative) consisting of seven.

REDONDA

Is a small island situated between Montserrat and Nevis; it is easy of access to ships but is entirely uninhabited.

NEVIS

Lies in 17° 10′ N. lat., 62° 42′ W. long. Its area is about twenty miles, a large mountain rising in the centre to the height of 2500 feet. The scenery of the island is very beautiful and its fertility remarkable.

Sir Thomas Warner founded a colony of our countrymen here in 1628, which progressed greatly, a few years later, under the administration of Governor Lake, "a knowing person and fearing God." Later in the seventeenth century its prosperity received several very severe checks. In the year 1706, a French expedition came down upon the island and committed great devastation there. In the year following its ruin was almost completed by a terrific hurricane, which desolated it from end to end. Commerce slowly revived in after years, sugar becoming the staple commodity, and being cultivated in place of ginger and tobacco.

So late as the year 1825, Coleridge comments upon the ill-treatment and wretched condition of the negro population in this island; these are evils which, we are thankful to be able to add, have almost disappeared since the act of negro emancipation.

The population of Nevis was estimated in 1707 to amount to 4780 in toto; it is now about 10,200; such at least was the estimate of the president of the island in the year 1851. The government consists of a representative assembly of nine, a council of seven members, and a president.

St. CHRISTOPHER'S OR St. KITT'S

Was so named by Columbus in the year 1493, its mountains bearing some fancied resemblance to the images of that saint; by the natives it is said to have been called the "Fertile Isle." St. Kitt's is about twenty miles in length, but with very small breadth; it is separated from Nevis by a narrow and dangerous channel. It has been compared in form to an outstretched leg, and has a ridge of lofty and volcanic mountains running like a back-bone through it. The climate is described as being of a dry and healthy character.

Some writers have claimed for St. Kitt's the honour of being the first territory in the West Indies colonised by Great Britain. The Spaniards certainly never took possession of the island, which is said to have been first settled in the year 1623, by Mr. Thomas Warner and fourteen other persons, who immediately set about the cultivation of tobacco there. Their enterprise was seriously checked soon after by a hurricane which swept over the island. Warner sailed to England, whence in a short time he returned, bearing with him valuable assistance both in men and the necessaries of life. About the same time the captain and crew of a French privateer landed on the island, where they were received with great kindness by our countrymen, among whom they appear to have settled down. The Europeans are said to have treated the native Caribs with great barbarity in an encounter with them shortly after this.

In the year 1629, the Spaniards asserted their right to the island of St. Kitt's, and with a powerful force suddenly fell upon the English and French inhabitants there. The French settlers quitted the island; the English generally fled to the mountains, but were obliged to surrender, and many were carried off to labour in the Spanish mines.

The English and French returned, however, on the departure of the Spaniards from St. Kitt's; internal strife seems to have become henceforth the bane of the colony, the emigrants of the two great nations not agreeing among themselves. These disputes were finally arranged at the Treaty of Utrecht (1714-15) when the island was ceded to Great Britain.

In the year 1782, St. Kitt's was invaded by the French and taken after a month's siege, during which a great destruction of life and property took place. It was restored by the Treaty of Versailles in the following year to England. In 1804, a terrible hurricane swept over the island, and in the following year, a French expedition invaded it, and extorted out of the fears of its inhabitants a contribution of 18,000*l.*, committing also great damage to some ships at anchor.

The population of St. Kitt's at the commencement of the last century was given as 5115; in 1844, it amounted to 23,430. The government consists of a representative assembly, a legislative and executive council, and a lieut.-governor.

ANGUILLA.

So named either from its peculiar shape, or from its being infested with snakes, is the most northern of the Caribbean group of islands, and is situated forty-five miles north-west of St. Kitt's. It is described as having a "pastoral aspect," the surface being for the most part flat and capable of great cultivation, though but little of it has been hitherto worked. There are several smaller islands lying in the vicinity.

Anguilla was settled by our countrymen in 1650, but its possession was for a long time disputed by the French. In 1745, the governor, Hodge, with a handful of militia defended the island gallantly against 600 Frenchmen. Subsequently, in the year 1796, the little colony there settled suffered very much from the ravages of Citoyen Victor Hugues and the French revolutionists; from that period it has been in comparative peace and prosperity. The population of Anguilla in 1724 was rated at 360 whites, and 900 negroes; total about 1260. In 1834, it was stated at 674 whites and free coloured; 2226 negro slaves; total 2920. The island is a dependency of St. Kitt's, to whose representative assembly it sends one member. The following satisfactory report was given by Governor Higginson in 1846. "The native inhabitants are a superior race, and particularly correct in their deportment. They are in comfortable circumstances, raise stock and provisions for their own consumption, and occasionally for exportation. Crime is almost unknown." *

THE VIRGIN ISLANDS

Were discovered by Columbus in 1493, and received their present name in honour of St. Ursula and the eleven thousand virgins of legendary renown. They lie north-west of the Caribbean islands, and are evidently connected with the lofty range of hills towards the eastern extremity of Cuba, which extend over a distance of some 1400 miles. The virgin group consists of about fifty small islets, they extend over a distance of twenty-four leagues east and west, and sixteen leagues north and south. Some of them are in the possession of Denmark, but the greater part belong to Great Britain, and of these the chief are Tortola, Virgin Gorda, and a few others. The characteristic features of the group are described to be rugged heights and precipitous coast lines, with numerous bays and creeks. There are tracts of land

---

* Annual Report on Blue Book, p. 44.

which afford excellent pasturage for cattle; of these the emancipated negroes are generally the proprietors.

The Virgin Islands were first occupied in 1648 by Dutch buccaneers, who established themselves at Tortola, and built a fort there. In Charles the Second's reign the group was wrested from its former masters by British adventurers, and in 1680 some English planters emigrated thither from Anguilla, and ere long established a thriving colony. The first representative assembly of this group met in the year 1774, and it is remarkable that they subjected themselves at once to the $4\frac{1}{2}$ per cent. impost, which had lain so heavily on some of the Windward Islands. This tax was abolished in 1838.

The population of the Virgin group is thus stated in 1720; whites 1122, blacks 1509; total 2631. In 1834, whites 800, free coloured 600, negro slaves 5135; total 6535. The government consists of a lieut.-governor, a council, and an assembly.

The conduct of the negroes since their emancipation in this colony has been described as orderly and industrious.

CHAP. VI.

THE BAHAMA AND BERMUDA ARCHIPELAGOS.

The Bahamas or Lucayos (the latter is their native name) constitute a large group of islands, long and narrow in form for the most part, and surrounded by innumerable coral reefs extending between the east coast of Florida and the island of Hayti. They are very low and flat, and in many parts capable of considerable cultivation.

The Bahama group was the first land which greeted the eyes of Columbus and his fellow-travellers in the New World. The inhabitants of these islands were very numerous, and of a gentle and friendly disposition; and it is sad to recount the cruelties to which they were subjected by those whom they received with open arms on their first landing. So hard were the burdens cast upon this unhappy race that the whole Bahama archipelago became ere long uninhabited, and remained in that condition until the year 1629, when New Providence was settled by the English, and continued to be held by them until 1641, when they were expelled in a very barbarous manner by the Spaniards. Our countrymen colonised the island again in 1666, but in 1703 they were once more driven away from it by a French and Spanish expedition. During the course of the last century the Bahamas became a terrible nest for pirates, buccaneers, &c.; and in order to put an end to their ravages the British government once more took possession of the colony. By the intrepid exertions of Captain Woodes Rogers, R.N., who was appointed governor in 1718, the pirates were eventually subdued, and peace restored to those regions.

In 1776 the Americans fitted out an expedition against our colony in New Providence. The whole Bahama group were confirmed to Great Britain by the Treaty of Versailles in 1783. Many loyalists came from the United States to settle in these islands at the conclusion of the American revolutionary war.

The population of the Bahamas in 1722 was given as follows:—830 whites, 310 blacks; total 1140. In 1851 it amounted to 6243 whites, 21,276 blacks; total 27,519. From these figures it may be concluded that the Bahamas have been a prosperous colony for many years past. The government consists of a governor, a council, and a representative assembly of seventeen members. The emancipated negroes here are reported as distinguished by habits of sobriety, order, and decency.

That portion of the Bahama group which is situated nearest Hayti, including Turk's Island and the Caicos, has been recently, at the request of its inhabitants, separated from the rest of the archipelago, and erected into a presidency under the control of the Governor of Jamaica. This settlement is described as in a prosperous condition.

THE BERMUDA ISLANDS.

These constitute a small archipelago lying in the midst of the North Atlantic Ocean, in 32° 20′ N. lat., 64° 30′ W. long. The nearest point of continental land is Cape Hatteras, in North Carolina, some 600 miles off. The islands are very numerous, being for the most part mere specks in the ocean; however, they are surrounded by a belt of coral reefs measuring about twenty-seven miles across. There is scarcely anything in the whole group deserving the name of an eminence, the highest point being only 250 feet above the level of the sea. Nevertheless, there are some very striking and beautiful points about the scenery of the Bermudas; and their climate is of a very mild, equable, and generally healthy nature.

The Bermuda Islands were discovered by a Spaniard in 1527, and were named after their discoverer. They have often proved true havens of refuge to shipwrecked mariners, who have constructed vessels of the cedar trees which grow there, and in these have contrived to reach the place of their destination in safety. A British settlement was formed in the Bermudas in

1641, by a brother of Sir George Somers, one of those who had been formerly wrecked on this shore. He brought with him about sixty persons, and it soon became a colony of considerable importance, as it must continue for ever to this country, having been called the key to our American territories. During the civil wars of England the Bermudas received a large accession of emigrants from the mother-country, many of whom returned, however, at the restoration of the monarchy.

During the war of American independence the Bermudas became a military and naval station of great importance, and several prize ships were brought into its harbours. The American government were eagerly anxious to wrest these islands from the grasp of England, but found them too strongly fortified, both by natural and artificial means, to give any hope to them of effecting their object. Since that period the defences of this colony have been rendered almost impregnable at considerable cost to the British government.

Here, as elsewhere in our West Indian colonies, great prejudice was excited in the minds of the white planters against any attempt on the part of the Wesleyan and other missionaries to forward the education religious, moral, and intellectual of their negro slaves. This circumstance seems to have led to several very disagreeable encounters towards the close of the last and commencement of the present century, in which missionary clergymen appear from time to time to have undergone more or less persecution. Of late years, however, the condition of the colony has been greatly improved in these respects; and it is one very satisfactory token of this improvement, that here, as in Antigua, at the period of emancipation, the "apprenticeship system" was cheerfully dispensed with on the part of the planters as being unnecessary.

The population of the Bermudas was stated in 1698 as 3615 whites, 2247 blacks; total 5862. In 1851 it amounted to 4669 whites, 6423 blacks; total 11,092. The legislature consists of a governor, a council of nine members, and a representative assembly of thirty-six members. Governor Elliott reported, in August 1852, that the progress of the colony "continued to be satisfactory, particularly in the rural industry of the people."

CHAP. VII.

HONDURAS AND OTHER DEPENDENCIES OF JAMAICA— BRITISH GUIANA—GENERAL REMARKS.

THE territory of Honduras is situated on the eastern coast of Central America, between 15° and 19° N. lat. and 88° and 90° W. long. Its length is about 200 and its breadth 100 miles, but the boundaries have never been defined very accurately, a circumstance which is the more to be regretted, as that part of the world has become of late years so plentiful a subject for international strife and controversy. The character of the country on the coast line, that part of it which has been best known hitherto, is low and flat, but as it recedes from the coast it becomes of a bolder character, rising gradually higher, and is watered by several fine rivers, particularly the Rio Hondo, which forms the northern boundary of the territory, and the Belize, on which is situated the head-quarters of the British settlement, the town of Belize. The climate is hot and moist towards the sea coast, but it has been much ameliorated of late years by the clearing away of underwood and the drainage of the soil. In the interior the climate is far more adapted to the European constitution than on the sea shore.

Columbus first sighted the territory of Honduras in 1502, having been directed thither by a fine canoe belonging to a cacique of those parts, which he encountered at a neighbouring island. The Spaniards described the country in question as at that time thickly inhabited, and that by a race of noble appearance, pleasant manners, and who spoke several different languages. Here, as elsewhere, the Golden Age of these simple tribes was speedily changed to a state of iron servitude under the uncompromising rule of Spain. The mines of Honduras are said to have been the grave of a million of native inhabitants; and when these were at length deserted for new and more promising ones the country had become almost depopulated.

The rich mahogany and other valuable products of its woods, never, however, proved an attraction to Europeans, and several Spanish settlements were formed along the coast during the course of the sixteenth and seventeenth centuries; but their progress was much obstructed by the inroads of the pirates of the neighbouring seas, among whom some of the most renowned characters have been Englishmen. Gage, who visited this country in 1630, speaks in high terms of the hospitality and kindness of the few remaining "poor Indians." The river and town of Belize have received their name from a famous buccaneer named Willis, who in 1638 settled on the banks of that river.

The English cause received great assistance in this part of the world from the Mosquito nation, who, with good reason, detested the very name of Spain, and in the year 1687, when the Duke of Albemarle was at Jamaica, actually sought to place themselves under the protection of the British crown. Sir Hans Sloane testifies to a memorial which he saw the Indians present to the Governor of Jamaica to the above effect. From that period they have professed a constant allegiance to the sovereign of Great Britain.

The occupation of the Honduras territory by England has obtained recognition in treaties with several foreign countries. In 1670 and in 1713 the Spanish government explicitly confirmed the right of Great Britain to the country in question. In 1717, however, a descent was made by them on Campeche, and much injury was done to the settlement formed there. At the Treaty of Paris in 1763 the Spanish government offered to guarantee the British settlers in these parts from molestation, on condition that all the fortified stations of Great Britain, both on the coast of Honduras and also on that of the Mosquito territory should be demolished. It is to be regretted that so unjust and exorbitant a demand was agreed to on the part of our government. During the period of peace which ensued Central America remained in a very unsettled state, and when they obtained knowledge of the recommencement of hostilities the Spaniards in these regions attacked with a considerable force the island called St. George's Cay, or Turneffe, about three leagues distant from Belize, and led a considerable number of persons thence as prisoners to Havanna. A British force, however, arriving at the scene of action, under Commodore Luttrell, retaliated upon the invaders with great success. At the peace of Versailles (1783), the British territory in Belize received a considerable accession with the consent of the Spanish government, but greatly to the indignation of her settlers in the colony of Yucatan and others bordering on the province in question. The Governor of Yucatan secretly prepared an armament which, in 1796, he embarked on board a flotilla of thirty-one vessels. Our colony at Belize had timely warning of this formidable expedition, and by the energy and zeal of the authorities combined with the bravery of the inhabitants scattered the enemy after an engagement of three hours' duration. From that period the colony of Belize has remained quietly in the possession of the British crown.

The Bay Islands, Ruatan, Bonacea, and other islets in the eastern part of the Gulf of Honduras, became British possessions during the course of the eighteenth century, and have since been peopled by the emigrations from the Caymans of the descendants of English buccaneers, who inhabited those islands. This race of men, produced chiefly by intercourse with African women, are said to be athletic, industrious, and of good moral character. They have a legislative assembly which, at their own request, is prorogued by the authority of the Governor of British Honduras. The present amount of the population is stated at some 2000 souls.

The Caymans are three small islands situated west of Jamaica. Thirty years ago their population was stated to be about 2000; since that period, however, the inhabitants, as above detailed, have emigrated in considerable numbers to Ruatan and the other Bay Islands, and the present population of the Caymans is consequently stated to amount only to a few hundreds.

There has lately been published, for the use of Parliament, a copy of the treaty between her Majesty and the republic of Honduras respecting the Bay Islands, the Mosquito Indians, and the rights and claims of British subjects. This treaty was signed at Comayagna on the 28th December 1839, and ratifications were exchanged at the same place on the 18th April 1860. By this treaty her Majesty agrees to recognise the islands of Ruatan, Guanaca, Elena, Utile, Barbarete, and Morat, known as the Bay Islands, as part of the republic of Honduras, the condition being, that they are never to be surrendered to any other nation or state whatsoever. A similar arrangement is made with regard to the British protectorate of the Mosquito territory, the condition being that Honduras shall grant 5000 dollars annually, for the next ten years, for the education of the Mosquito Indians.

BRITISH GUIANA.

This fine colony extends between the rivers Amazon and Orinoco, from 8° 40′ N. lat. to 3° 30′ S. lat., from 50° to 68° W. long., and its area covers some 100,000 square miles. It possesses considerable variety of soil and climate, the inland territory being more or less mountainous and elevated, while along the whole Atlantic coast, which stretches for 300 miles along the north, there is a fine alluvial tract formed entirely by the deposition of matter into the bed of the ocean by the four fine rivers which run along its territory from south to north. These rivers are the Essequibo, the Demerara, the Berbice, and the Corentyn, the last of which forms the boundary between British Guiana and Dutch Guiana. None of them are navigable for large craft to any great distance from their mouth, the principal barrier in each case being the prevalence of cataracts, some of which are of vast size and imposing appearance.

The alluvial portion of British Guiana is the only one which has been hitherto submitted to cultivation; it is scarcely elevated above the sea level, and is drained, like the Netherlands, by a system of canals and sluices, dykes being raised to prevent the incursions of the sea. We are informed by Sir W. Raleigh that the aboriginal inhabitants, whom he terms a bold and hardy race, lived during the rainy season in huts built upon the trees, in order to shelter themselves from the effects of the overflowing of the rivers.

The principal towns of British Guiana are Georgetown and New Amsterdam, both flourishing settlements; there are scarcely any others in the whole colony which as yet merit more than the name of villages. There appear to be no reliable statements with reference to the population of this noble colony until within the last thirty years or so. In 1831, the white population is given at 3529; the free coloured at 7521; and the slaves at 89,484; total 100,526. In 1834, after the emancipation, the population had fallen to 92,943. In 1851, it stood thus:—whites 11,558; coloured 116,137; total 127,695. This estimate does not include the aboriginal Indians living in the interior of the country. These are estimated to amount to some 7000.

Guiana seems to have been first visited by Europeans in the shape of Jesuit missionaries, who spent several years there preaching to the natives, until about the year 1579 A.D., when they were driven away by the Dutch, who for the next two hundred years were the principal occupants of that noble country. In the year 1621 A.D., the Dutch West India Company was embodied and invested with very extensive privileges over the Dutch possessions on the South American main. In 1720, a company called the Berbice Association was formed, whose principal duties were the cultivation of sugar, cocoa, and indigo, and moreover to raise money for the purchase of slaves. This company was in 1732 invested with the power of appointing a governor and council of six persons to administer the affairs of the colony of Berbice. Towards the middle of the last century, European settlers began to penetrate somewhat more into the interior of the country, and it was about that period that the alluvial lands and the banks of the rivers Demerara and Essequibo had settlements formed upon them. In the year 1763, a formidable slave insurrection broke out in the colony of Berbice which, however, with the assistance of some British forces sent from Barbadoes by Admiral Douglas, was ere long quelled, when the wretched survivors of the movement, to the number of some hundreds, were barbarously put to death.

A short time after this occurrence, a return was made of the population of this colony, which stated the number of the whites at 116, and that of the negro slaves at 3370. In 1773-4, the town of Stalrock was formed at the mouth of the Demerara river which, under the name of Georgetown, is the present capital of British Guiana. In 1780, the Dutch having joined the crusade in favour of American liberty, Demerara and Essequibo were captured by the British Admiral Lord Rodney, but were subsequently recaptured by the French, and restored to their former possessors, the Dutch, at the close of the war.

The three colonies of Demerara, Essequibo, and Berbice were once more captured by Great Britain in the year 1796; they were restored to the Dutch at the peace of Amiens in 1802, but war having broken out again in the following year, they were recaptured by our countrymen, and have since that period remained British possessions.

In 1823, advices were sent out from the home government to Major-General Murray, the Lieut-Governor of British Guiana, with reference to "ameliorating the condition of the slave population, and preparing them for freedom." A rumour on the subject of their projected emancipation ere long began to circulate among the negroes in this colony, and is said to have been inflamed by certain persons who represented that the governor and the planters alone stood in the way of their entire liberation. The consequence was a very general rising of the slaves, by which the planters were so surprised that most of them were overpowered and placed in the stocks. It must be added, however, to the honour of the negroes, that scarcely a single act of violence is recorded on their part during the brief period of their triumph. They were soon dispersed by the arrival of the regular troops, and we blush to record the fact that they were treated with most inhuman barbarity on the part of their enraged masters. It would have been well if the vengeance of the planters had stopped even here; but we regret to add that, as in Jamaica, and elsewhere, the missionaries who were labouring among the slave population were charged with having secretly incited them to insurrection; whereas on the contrary, it was owing to their mild exhortations that so little violence had been committed on the part of the blacks. On the present occasion, the vengeance of the dominant party fell principally on the Rev. J. Smith, who was tried for his life by a court-martial and condemned to death, but recommended to the mercy of the crown. The cruel treatment which he experienced in prison after this sentence speedily brought his life to a close. Very general indignation was raised when the account of these proceedings arrived in England, but there can be little doubt that circumstances of this character were greatly instrumental in opening the eyes of the people of this country to the demoralising influences of slavery.

In 1833, on the eve of the great change which was to be operated on the negro population, Sir James Carmichael Smyth was appointed lieut.-governor of

British Guiana. He inaugurated his administration by restoring the liberty of the press, which had been partially withdrawn a few years previously. His well known friendliness to the cause of negro emancipation made him the victim of a great deal of abuse on the part of the planting interest. So strongly impressed, however, were the black population with the sincerity of his sympathies in their favour, that in the year 1834, after the apprenticeship system had commenced, his mere presence on the spot and exhortations were sufficient to disperse a formidable band of some 600 men, who had collected in order to obtain by violence that freedom of which they still considered that they were likely to be deprived by underhand means. Sir J. C. Smyth's conduct obtained the full approbation of the home government, and he received from the sovereign, in December 1837, a full commission as governor instead of his former title of lieut.-governor. This worthy man was enabled to effect in the course of a few years, several important reforms in the administration of the government in British Guiana, but to the distress of all parties, for his worth had by that time become generally appreciated, he was carried off by a sudden illness shortly before that most important epoch in our colonial history, the 1st August 1838.

It is much to be regretted that the planters in Guiana neglected to make suitable preparations for the great event of the total emancipation of the negroes. Instead of preparing for the modified intercourse which would ensue between themselves and their former slaves, they chose to make some absurd regulations to counteract apprehended violence on the part of the negroes. The result proved the utter uselessness of these measures, for when the great day at length arrived, it was passed by the blacks almost entirely in thanksgiving and prayer in every part of this vast and important colony.

Since that important epoch a considerable amount of property has passed into the hands of the black population in Guiana. Up to the end of 1848, 446 estates had been thus acquired by their united subscriptions, and the properties in question divided among the subscribers, 10,541 houses being built on them, which were inhabited by 44,443 persons.

. . . .

A century ago the West Indies formed a portion of our colonial empire, which ranked second to no other in importance and general prosperity. The great "West India Interest," composed principally and indeed almost entirely of the owners of thriving plantations in sugar and the various productions for which these countries have been famous, exercised its influence in the Imperial Legislature and in the Cabinet, equally with, at times even more prominently than the North American colonies or the East India Company, while the planters themselves resided chiefly in the mother-country, spending their princely fortunes with open hand, and mingling with all that was most illustrious in rank and talent there. Even at this early period, however, the symptoms of fatal decay were seriously developed in the social and political system upon which our West Indian colonies had been established, and these did not fail to grow up year by year, and entwine themselves ever more closely around it, until the judgment of mankind cried out against the evil, and it became necessary to pluck up the tree by its very roots.

In truth, while these great proprietors scattered their wealth in England and elsewhere, they left their estates in the hands of overseers and book-keepers, a class of men by whom the poor cultivators of the soil, the negro slaves, were treated with great injustice and severity. On the other hand, the negroes themselves—the victims of the most dreadful species of wrong which any portion of our race have ever undergone from the hands of their fellow-men—who shall paint the utter degradation and wretchedness of their position in our colonies? And this under the flag of England, which has ever prided herself on being the friend of freedom, and the refuge of the distressed among mankind. The "Code Noir," or Negro Code of Jamaica and our other West Indian colonies, has obtained a barbarous celebrity from its unreasonable, not to say inhuman strictness.

The peace of these flourishing settlements was, moreover, constantly liable to be broken by insurrections among the slaves, who, whenever they surprised their masters unprepared and unarmed by these sudden movements, felt little remorse, we fear, in exacting a dreadful return for all the oppression to which they had been subjected. These insurrections followed one another, almost with regularity, after an average interval of a few years, and it was impossible that any great feeling of security could exist in a society thus constituted.

This earlier phase of our West Indian colonies was already in the last stage of decay, when the slumber of nations was awakened from its profound repose in every part of the world by the occurrences of the French revolution. The principles and maxims of that feverish period were not long in finding their way to the West Indies, and in penetrating there among the negro population, first in the French settlements, but afterwards more or less among those of the other European nations. The last ten years of the eighteenth century, and the first twenty or so of the present, comprised a period of visionary ideas and impalpable schemes, broached by ardent though not always scrupulous minds. It is not wonderful, therefore, if the design of William Wilberforce and his colleagues for the emancipation of the negro race in America and the West Indies should be looked on by many sober persons as only calculated to rank among the airy visions of that excitable period. As such it was long treated by many wise and well disposed individuals, but those who advocated it flinched not from their purpose, and after a long and wearisome struggle, this great measure was carried, the nation entailing on itself thereby an additional debt of some 20,000,000*l.* in amount. As we write at present six and twenty years have rolled by since the ever memorable session in which Parliament sanctioned and passed the great measure of negro emancipation, and we wish here in a few words to express our opinion as to the results which have followed that important act.

It is not to be denied that the interests of the European proprietors or planters, who formed the aristocracy in those regions during the "good old times of slavery," have lamentably declined in all our West Indian colonies; in Jamaica the total number of white inhabitants is now less than a third of its former amount. But then we have the reverse side of the picture. In place of some few thousand Europeans who formerly divided the country between them, there are now in Jamaica alone 100,000 proprietors of small estates and farms, and these, with very few exceptions, are negroes.

It must not be overlooked, moreover, that a good

deal of the misfortunes which have overtaken our West Indian colonies of late years have been the result of change in our commercial system, from the introduction of a free trade policy. The evils in question will, however, prove, we hope, to be of a partial and temporary nature; and, meanwhile, it is impossible not to contemplate with joy and satisfaction the prospect of a race, so recently the most degraded among the human species, improving year after year in civilisation, in refinement, and by all accounts, in intellectual vigour and enlightenment.

Among other results of a similar tendency, it is particularly worth remarking the constantly increasing intercourse between the black population of the West Indies and their brethren on the vast continent of Africa, the common home of their race, especially towards the civilised settlements on the western coast, which have been founded under the patronage of enlightened governments, as Sierra Leone and Liberia. When we consider that the West Indian negroes have now for many years been constantly rising in the scale of education, general enlightenment, and the arts of social life, it seems impossible not to comprehend a great significance in this increasing movement towards intercourse with their less favoured brethren, and to breathe an earnest hope that the sons of Africa may ere long emerge from the darkness of ages, and take their stand among the civilised nations of the earth.

SECTION IV.

AFRICA, AND ISLANDS OF THE ATLANTIC.

CHAPTER I.

PROGRESS OF AFRICAN DISCOVERY, SETTLEMENTS ON THE NORTH-WEST COAST, AND REMARKS ON THE AFRICAN SLAVE TRADE.

THE great continent of Africa has been celebrated from the earliest times; it was there that in the infancy of our race the marvels of Egypt were constructed, these monuments of skill and enterprise which still remain to astonish us, and exercise our ingenuity in vainly attempting to solve the riddle of their origin; it was thence that the republic of Carthage, the greatest maritime state of antiquity, and the rival of Imperial Rome herself, extended her commerce from the shores of Britain to the far east, with its fabulous stores of wealth. On this continent it was, moreover, that at a later period of history the successors of the Arabian prophet Mohammed pursued their conquests, extending their vast empire in a north-westerly direction, until they had crossed the Straits of Gibraltar even, and established a footing in Christian Europe itself. Since this latter period, about the ninth or tenth centuries of our era, Africa has become the most stationary of all the great divisions of the globe with reference to the progress of civilisation and social reform, or rather it may be said in some parts to have receded sadly from the position which it then occupied in these respects. Brighter days are yet, however, it may be confidently hoped, in reserve for this long degraded portion of the globe; the greatest and most enlightened nations of Europe, France and England, the one in the north the other in the south of Africa, are directing their energies to civilise and improve that vast continent, supposed to contain not less than 150,000,000 of human beings, sunk for the most part in the darkest state of ignorance and barbarism.

The ancients appear to have been well acquainted with the whole line of the northern coast of this great continent; on the western side they penetrated probably no farther than Cape Verd and the adjacent islands; on the eastern coast, however, they certainly penetrated some way beyond the equinoctial line, and it has been generally conjectured that Sofala, opposite the island of Madagascar, is the same with the Ophir mentioned in the Old Testament. During the period of Arabian domination in the north of Africa, that *then* enterprising people advanced a considerable distance into the interior of the continent, and on the western coast, where several important settlements were established by them between the tenth and fourteenth centuries. About the close of this period the European nations generally became excited by a strong desire to explore the hitherto unknown regions of the world; and among the most important subjects of discussion at the time was the mystery which still, as of old, enveloped the southern portion of the African continent. The discovery of the compass had rendered the caution of mariners in not venturing out of sight of land no longer necessary; and accordingly it was at this period (towards the close of the fifteenth century), that those discoveries were made in both hemispheres, which have changed the fate of the world.

In the first rank of the promoters of geographical discovery and science generally, must be placed the name of Prince Henry of Portugal, who flourished during the fifteenth century of our era, though it must be added, that he has been branded as one of the first authors, if not the very first, of the infamous traffic in negro slaves. As the history of the slave trade is closely connected with that of our settlements in Africa, it may be well to insert a few statements relative to the rise and progress of that dreadful system. Prince Henry, and others among its early promoters, professed themselves to be incited by the desire of converting these poor heathen to the Christian faith, and for this purpose encouraged a regular system of "kidnapping" the natives on the part of the captains of vessels cruising on the African coast. This system of kidnapping was, however, very soon discovered to be so profitable to those engaged in it, that it was indulged in to an enormous extent, native chiefs being enticed to make war on one another, in order to sell the captives, whom they might thus acquire to European slave dealers.* In the mean time discovery was rapidly proceeding along the coast of Africa, and at length, through the exertions of Prince Henry, the old notion of western Europe, that the torrid zone was a region of which the heat was insupportable to human life became thoroughly dissipated, and towards the close of the fifteenth century, Bartholomew Diaz, Vasco de Gama, and others, passing the equinoctial line in triumph sailed as far as the Cape of Good Hope, the southern point of the continent. Diaz appears to have doubled this celebrated promontory for the first time in 1486, a circumstance which was ere long followed by the discovery of the entire route to India by the Atlantic and Indian Oceans. This latter object was effected by Vasco de Gama about the year 1497 A.D.

* The statements on this subject are derived from well-known works written by the friends of the abolition of slavery, as Bandinel " On Slavery," Clarkson " On the Slave Trade," &c. &c.

The discovery of America by Columbus in 1492 gave a new impulse to the African slave trade, the first cargo of negroes being introduced into the island of St. Domingo in 1503. From this time the abominable traffic increased at a fearfully rapid ratio, 12,000 being the annual amount sold in the market of Lisbon about the year 1539. Even at that early period the traffic in human beings was denounced by many good and great men; but the immense profit arising from it to those more immediately engaged, and the false notions which then generally prevailed on subjects of moral and political philosophy, proved powerful enough, in spite of their indignant denunciations, to buoy up this hateful system.

At first, Portugal was the only country which enjoyed the profits of the "carrying" system, as it was called, i. e., the kidnapping of negroes, and conveying them to America and elsewhere to be sold. Gradually, however, most, if not all the nations of Europe, were drawn into a participation of it, and in consequence, established forts and settlements along the north-west coast of the African continent, a region which no other inducement than the desire of gain, would assuredly have led them to occupy, as it is well known to be most destructive to the life of Europeans, and the inhabitants of the north generally. The principal states of Europe which have settlements of this nature, are at present England, France, Spain, Portugal, and Holland; Denmark, also, formerly occupied several military stations with tracts of land attached to them along the coast of Guinea, which were purchased from her by Great Britain in 1850 for 10,000*l.*

The infamous traffic in human flesh was, however, towards the close of the last and commencement of the present century, through the efforts of philanthropic men, and latterly from the general cry of civilised Europe and America, denounced by all the Christian governments in the world, and great sums of money have been expended by Great Britain in the humane attempt utterly to destroy and root it out. Up to the present moment, however, all these efforts have enjoyed only a partial success. A large contraband trade is still carried on annually on both the eastern and western coasts of the African continent, and we are informed that some of the powers, among whom the names of Spain and Portugal are conspicuous, have violated every pledge which they have given on the subject, and up to the present time contrive to foment, in an underhand manner, that traffic, which they have actually received the bounties of this country to assist them in the work of its overthrow.* The amount of casualties which take place during every voyage of a slave ship across the Atlantic with a cargo of human victims, is frightful to contemplate; from a comparison of the various years between 1798 and 1847, it has been com-

* M. Martin, Book III. chap. i. p. 172.

puted at 25 per cent. In the year 1847, 84,356 is the number of unhappy negroes recorded as having been exported from the African shores; of this number, only 63,267 lived to see the opposite coast, making the amount of casualties 21,089. The above statement does not include those negroes who are carried off to be sold in the Mussulman states of Turkey, Persia, and Northern Africa generally, and which are computed at some 50,000 annually. On the whole, it may be said that great efforts are still required on the part of civilised nations in order to extinguish the slave trade effectually, and introduce a better order of things among the desolate tribes of that benighted portion of the earth.

THE GAMBIA RIVER.

The most northern settlements possessed by Great Britain on the west coast of Africa, are toward the mouth of this great river, the principal of these being the town of Bathurst on Saint Mary's Island, just at its entrance. At first this settlement had a very bad reputation for unhealthiness, but of late years, by the efforts of the government, it has become greatly improved in this respect, and the mortality for five years previous to 1849, having amounted to only 4·40 per cent. of the population. A very extensive commerce is already entered upon with Europe and America in the "Ground Nut," a product of these parts, and it is rapidly increasing. As a natural consequence, traces of civilisation are beginning to appear among the native population, which is rapidly multiplying in this part of the continent. "Already," says the enterprising governor, Mr. Macdonnel, "a community of commercial interests has begun to bind together the various tribes which people the banks of the Gambia, for a distance of 400 miles from its mouth."* The chiefs of this territory are moreover becoming alive to the circumstance that by making war on one another, they only drive away from their land profitable tenants, whose pursuits require more than five months of leisure to till the ground, and gather up its produce.

South of the Gambia river, Great Britain claims two settlements, the island of Balama, and those called the Isles de Loss: the former, however, is not occupied, and the latter seems, from the unhealthy nature of the climate scarcely available for Europeans.

SIERRA LEONE.

This celebrated settlement is situated on a peninsula, which extends about thirty-three miles along the shore of the Atlantic Ocean, the northern boundary of the colony being the Mungo River, in 8° 50′ N. lat.; its confines on the south and east sides, appear to have been not very clearly defined hitherto. The peninsula is traversed by a ridge of rocky mountains, some of

* Blue Book, 1852.

which attain the height of 2500 feet above the level of the sea; it also contains some level country, some of which is of a very swampy nature.

Sierra Leone, or Lion Mountain, was probably thus named by the Portuguese, who first discovered it in the year 1463, from the number of lions found in the neighbouring territory. From that period it became a celebrated resort for slave dealers of the various nations of Europe; among others, England had a slave-factory established here. In 1652, Sir John Hawkins, whose name is conspicuous even in the infamous annals of the slave trade, made a descent on this country, which he is said to have first laid waste, and afterwards carried off several hundreds of natives, to be conveyed to the West Indies and sold as slaves there.

During the later years of the eighteenth century, the benevolent idea was formed by several persons in this country, of providing a home in Africa itself for those negroes who were rescued from the horrors of the slave trade, or such as had been brought to England, where they were declared by Lord Chief Justice Mansfield, to be at once free. During the American war of independence, moreover, a considerable number of negroes served in the British army and navy, who, at the conclusion of that contest were disbanded, some of them being sent to Nova Scotia and the Bahamas, while a great many remained in England, itself in a state of great destitution. A committee of benevolent persons was formed to administer relief to the poor creatures, and about the same time a plan was proposed by a Dr. Smeathman, for the formation of a colony of free negroes at Sierra Leone, the principal motive for which plan being the circumstance, that many of the negroes had been originally carried away from that part of Africa, whence it was reasonably supposed that its climate would prove salubrious to themselves or their descendants. The English government entered readily into the scheme, and at their expense, more than 400 negroes were transported to the west African coast in the spring of the year 1787. On their arrival thither Captain Thomson, who commanded the expedition, purchased a tract of land on the peninsula of Sierra Leone, from the native chiefs of the neighbouring country, whither the colonists were landed and a settlement planned. This first attempt was, however, not very successful; the arrangements of the government were not well formed, and in the course of a year from their first setting out, the population of the new colony had, from various causes, dwindled down to one-half, and it was perhaps saved from entire destruction by the benevolent exertions of one individual, Mr. Granville Sharpe, who sent out a brig laden at his own expense, with a variety of articles which were urgently needed by the poor emigrants. Two years after, in 1789, another calamity befel the colony, a native chief invading it, and setting fire to the newly built town. A new town was subsequently founded, named Granville, a few miles from the former town. In 1791, the Sierra Leone Company was incorporated by Act of Parliament, and among its members included the names of Messrs. Granville Sharpe, Wilberforce, and Clarkson; its capital amounted to 250,000*l*. Emigrants now continued to flow into the settlement from various quarters, 1135 negroes being transported at their own request thither from Nova Scotia. The settlement of Freetown was now founded on an entirely new site, and has ever since been regarded as the capital of Sierra Leone.

In 1794, a most singular invasion of the peninsula took place on the part of a French flotilla, which approached the harbour of our settlement with the English flag hoisted, and having effected an entrance, committed great ravages, which it cost the company subsequently some 50,000*l*. to repair. This expedition is supposed to have been undertaken without the knowledge of the French government (with whom this country was, however, at war), and fitted out at the expense of some persons interested in the continuance of the slave trade, to which they foresaw the existence of a free negro colony on the African coast must ultimately prove a great blow.

The Sierra Leone Company did their best to repair this sad work of devastation, and by their efforts, combined with those of the colonists, Freetown arose once more from its ruins, and in the course of a few years was once more a flourishing settlement. About the commencement of the present century, the settlers on the territory of Sierra Leone were brought to a great state of despondency from internal dissensions, and marauding expeditions from time to time on the part of the native chiefs in the neighbourhood. In consequence of these circumstances, a parliamentary inquiry was made into the affairs of the colony, the result of which was, that in 1808 the administration of Sierra Leone was transferred from the company to the Crown. It appears, however, that before its dissolution, the company had signed treaties of peace with the native chiefs, and that it left the colony in a reviving condition of prosperity generally.

The population of Sierra Leone, when the settlement was first planned about the close of the last century, amounted only, as we have seen, to a few hundreds; in 1818, it had risen to 9,567; in 1836, it numbered 37,463; and in 1851, it amounted to 44,501. This increase is not very large, however, when it is considered that thousands of negroes, liberated from captured slave ships, have been landed on the shore of Sierra Leone during the course of this century, besides other sources, as immigration of negroes from the West Indies, and the British North American colonies. On the whole, then, it would appear, that almost an equal number of inhabitants have quitted Sierra Leone of late years, as have come to settle there in the same period; the point to which the emigrants thence have bent their course being chiefly the British West Indies. It is asserted, however, that from drainage and other results of its becoming the abode of civilised man, the climate of this country has been much less noxious of late years, even to European constitutions. On the whole, we would conclude with the earnest hope, that a settlement which is calculated to have so good an effect in civilising, by contact in commercial and other methods, the savage tribes who inhabit these vast countries may have a long and prosperous career.

CHAP. II.

THE GOLD COAST AND ISLANDS IN THE ATLANTIC OCEAN.

GREAT BRITAIN has under her control a territory of about two hundred and eighty miles in length on the Gold Coast of Africa, which extends inland as far as the confines of the kingdom of Ashantee. Some years since, the population of this territory was stated to be 280,500, and is steadily increasing. The attention of the European nations was drawn to this region by a prospect of a traffic in gold as well as slaves, and it is to this circumstance, doubtless, that the names of Gold Coast and Guinea (for the country in the interior) are to be attributed. The Portuguese founded the settlement of Cape Coast Castle in 1610, but were driven away thence soon after by the Dutch. In 1661, Cape Coast Castle was captured by our countrymen under Admiral Holmes, and having been confirmed to England by the treaty of Breda, in 1672, has remained in her possession ever since. Several other forts have been established from time to time along the Gold Coast by the African companies, whose privileges extended over this territory, which has been found of great value in the hands of England since the commencement of the present century for the suppression of the slave trade, of which this region was formerly one of the principal centres.

The British settlements on the Gold Coast have encountered rather a formidable neighbour in the Ashantees, a brave and warlike nation, said to number more than 4,000,000, whose government is an hereditary monarchy. This nation is rendered remarkable in history, from the fact, that they were the first who resolutely resisted the spread of the Mohammedan faith in the African continent, and were in consequence routed out of their original home among the Kong Mountains, whence they emigrated in a northerly direction to the neighbourhood of the Gold Coast, where they now occupy a considerable territory, their principal town being Kumasi, which is about a hundred and thirty miles direct from Cape Coast Castle. One of their kings, named Ozai Apoko, while engaged in subduing the adjoining tribe of Akim in the year 1731, obtained possession of certain "Notes," so called, which were said to have been given by the English company to the native chiefs on their first establishing forts along the coast. According to the tenor of these documents, the company, instead of purchasing territory, hired a certain portion for its own use, while they gave promissory notes to the chiefs for the regular payment of the rent. The other European companies appear to have held their territories in the same manner, and on the conquest of the tribes Akim, Asim, and Bonromy by the King of Ashantee, he obtained possession of the notes, upon which he claimed payment by "right of conquest" from the English, Dutch, and Danish companies, who had forts at Elmina and Occra, which claim was duly accorded to him by them.*

The English authorities appear to have acted with but little discretion on several occasions when brought into contact with the king and people of Ashantee. Our first war with them was in the year 1807, in consequence of the English governor taking the part of the Asim and Fantee chiefs, whose territories had been invaded by Ozai Jutu Quamina, the reigning monarch of Ashantee. All the efforts of the governor of the fort of Annamaboo, Mr. White, were ineffectual to preserve the chiefs in whose cause he had engaged from the hands of the conquering nation; and after having been himself severely wounded, and the castle of Annamaboo almost reduced to destruction, he concluded a treaty with Ozai Jutu Quamina, among the conditions of which were the surrender of Chibbu, Aputui, the other chief, having been so fortunate as to make his escape. Chibbu is said, to our great disgrace, to have been put to death with the most agonising tortures. It was also acknowledged by Colonel Torrane, the Governor-General, who came from Cape Coast Castle to hold a

* Bowditch's "Mission to Ashantee," p. 234.

conference with the King of Ashantee, that the whole territory of Fantee was the property of that monarch; and at the same time the arrears of rent for the lands belonging to Annamaboo and Cape Coast Castle were promised payment.

In the year 1821, the English African Company at the Gold Coast was dissolved, and its powers and privileges merged into the crown. About the same time there were several serious misunderstandings between the Ashantee government and the British authorities in the neighbourhood. In these transactions the conduct of our officials from time to time appears to bear little or no justification. On one occasion they went so far as to prevent the embarkation of a friendly embassy which the King of Ashantee had deputed to the Prince Regent, and which was to have been conveyed to England by British vessels of war. Mr. Dupuis, however, a gentleman who had played an important part in the negotiations with Ashantee, and who utterly disapproved of the line of conduct pursued by the British authorities, returned to England to represent the true state of things to the government there, first sending a message to the king, urgently entreating him to wait the result of his friendly exertions.

In March, 1822, Sir Charles M'Carthy arrived to take the government of the English settlements on the Gold Coast into his hands. He appears to have been very much in the dark as to the validity of the claims of the King of Ashantee on our government, and, furthermore, as to the real power of that barbarian chief. In consequence, he engaged rashly in war for the defence of the Fantees, and marched inland with a very small body of men, and very ill provided with stores and ammunition, to the Prah river, where he encountered the force of the enemy. The engagement that ensued was long sustained with desperate courage on both sides: but at length the enemy crossed the river at some distance above the field of battle and surprised our troops in the flank and in the rear. The small force was literally cut to pieces, Sir Charles with his principal officers being among the slain. Some time afterwards Cape Coast Castle itself was besieged by an army of Ashantees, and its garrison brought to a state of great distress. The enemy was, however, obliged at length to retire in consequence of the ravages of disease in their camp. In the month of September, 1826, a battle was fought between the Ashantees on the one hand and the Fantees, assisted by their English allies on the other. In the action, which proved decisive, the enemy suffered a severe defeat. Sir Neil Campbell, who was appointed about that time Governor-General on the Gold Coast, bent all his efforts towards the conclusion of peace with the Ashantee government, and at length succeeded in laying the foundation of an amicable settlement, although much hindered in his good designs by the Fantee chiefs, who were very much afraid of their interests being neglected. It was some years before any definite arrangement was concluded; when this took place, however, the King of Ashantee appears to have expressly abandoned his claim to the territory of the tribes near the coast.* Soon after a son and nephew of the king were sent to Great Britain, where they received an English education. Several missionaries have taken up their residence of late at Kumasi, the capital of the Ashantee monarchy. A special embassy was sent by the Queen of England to Kumasi in 1848, which was received and entertained by the king in a style of great though perhaps barbarian splendour. We may trust that the foundation has been laid in this quarter for the permanent improvement of the interior of Africa in civilisation and the arts of peace.

THE ISLANDS OF ASCENSION AND ST. HELENA.

These are two small islands situated in the midst of the South Atlantic Ocean. Ascension lies in lat. 7° 55′ S., long. 14° 25′ W., it is of volcanic origin, with scarcely a trace of verdure in any part of it. A coal depôt has been established there for facilitating the steam traffic through the South Atlantic Ocean.

* Dr. Beecham's "Ashantee and the Gold Coast," p. 68.

St. Helena is situated in lat. 15° 55′ S. and long. 5° 44′ W., above a thousand miles distant from the African Continent. Its length is ten miles and a half, its breadth six miles and three-quarters. Its total area is said to comprise 30,000 acres.

This island was discovered by Juan de Nova Castella, a Portuguese, in the year 1502, and was named by him in honour of the day on which he first sighted St. Helena. It is said to have been uninhabited by any other than seals and other amphibious animals. The Portuguese long concealed among themselves the existence of this island; it was, nevertheless, discovered by Captain Cavendish in the year 1588. This gentleman states that the Portuguese had built quite a settlement on the island, and that they had imported plenty of live stock thither. In the year 1645, the Dutch took formal possession of the island, the Portuguese having relinquished it some time before for their settlements on the western coast of Africa. The Dutch, however, abandoned St. Helena for the Cape of Good Hope in 1651, and it was then speedily taken possession of by a British fleet returning from the East Indies. The island was, moreover, admitted within the territories included under the East India Company's Charter, and it became ere long a somewhat flourishing settlement. In 1672 the Dutch contrived to gain possession of the island by a night surprise, but were expelled again in the following year by a British squadron under Captain

Munden, who succeeded in conveying thither some valuable prizes belonging to nations with whom we were then at war. In the year 1833, the Charter of the East India Company having been altered and considerably abridged, the Island of St. Helena passed to the possession of the crown. It was on this island that Napoleon Bonaparte was condemned to pass the latter years of his life in almost solitary confinement at Longwood, where he died on the 6th of May, 1821.

CHAP. III.

THE CAPE OF GOOD HOPE.

This important promontory remained for a considerable time after its discovery unclaimed by any of the European nations. The Portuguese, during the brief period of their naval prosperity, frequently made use of the bays in its neighbourhood to anchor their fleets, going towards and returning from the East Indies, for the purpose of recruiting their stores of provision, but they fell under the yoke of Philip the Second of Spain in the year 1581, and from that period may be dated their decline. About the same time, however, another small nation was engaged in throwing off the intolerable yoke of Spain, and establishing its fame as a great military people both by sea and land in every quarter of the globe. This was the Republic of the Netherlands, the history of whose gallant resistance to the proud autocrat of Spain, whose yoke they succeeded in breaking effectually at last, is worthy to be placed side by side with the most glorious achievements of classical antiquity.

The immediate cause of the Dutch settling at the Cape of Good Hope is very singular. The Haerlem, a vessel belonging to their East India Company, was wrecked off the South African coast in the year 1648, and two members of its crew found shelter on shore for several months, until the arrival of the next homeward bound vessels. They employed their time meanwhile in addressing a memorial to the directors of the East India Company in Holland, in which they set forth the advantages which might be expected from the establishment of a regular settlement at the Cape of Good Hope, and the excellence of its climate, as well as the peaceful nature of the aboriginal inhabitants. In consequence of this representation, the directors at once set on foot a settlement, at the head of which was placed a commander, J. Van Riebeeck. The expedition for this purpose sailed from Holland about the close of the year 1651, and appears to have consisted of about seventy or eighty persons, among whom were several convicts. The settlers were landed on April 24th of the ensuing year, and then was set on foot the humble beginnings of Cape Town, now a flourishing and handsome city. That these enterprising persons must have gone through very severe sufferings in the effort of laying the foundation of this great colony is very evident; those sufferings were, however, greatly aggravated by the false system which from the first they had adopted in their intercourse with the natives. Instead of meeting these with open hand and making them sincere and lasting allies, they appear to have adopted the vicious principle of getting "as much out of them as they could;" and on various occasions they made the unfortunate natives feel the severity of their hand to punish them. This line of conduct produced ere long a feeling of hostility on the part of the natives, and before ten years had elapsed from the foundation of the colony, the first "commando" or military expedition sallied forth from Cape Town against them.

In 1672, a contract was agreed upon between the native chiefs and the authorities of Cape Town, according to which the adjoining district was sold to the latter, a few baubles and other trifling things being all that was asked for on the part of the natives: however, as it has been observed, this was a step in the right direction, inasmuch as by it "was acknowledged the absence of any inherent right, on the part of the white race, to take forcible possession of the country of the coloured."

The conduct of the Dutch authorities at the Cape during the greater part of the eighteenth century, cannot be reviewed without a feeling of disgust, and at times even of horror. They appear to have set on foot almost regularly every year the "commandoes" or military expeditions against the Hottentots and Bosjesmans or Bush people, in which hundreds of men, women, and children were ordinarily slaughtered on the part of the natives, while the marauders scarcely lost one man. It is apparent that the real object of these murderous expeditions was to chase the natives entirely out of their original haunts, and drive them further and further into the interior.* Mr. Maynier stated before the British commissioners, in 1824, that on being appointed Landrost of Graaf Reynet, in the year 1792, " he found that regularly every year large commandoes, consisting of two hundred or three hundred armed boors, had been sent against the Bosjesmen, and learnt by their reports that generally many hundreds of Bosjesmen were killed by them, amongst which number there were perhaps not more than six or ten men escaped, and that the greatest part of the killed comprised helpless women and innocent children. I was also made acquainted with the most horrible atrocities committed on those occasions, such as ordering the Hottentots to dash out against the rocks the brains of infants, too young to be carried off by the farmers for the purpose of using them as bondsmen, in order to save powder and shot." †

---

* Some very sad statements on these subjects, and on the general condition of the colony during the latter part of the last century, are to be found in Thunberg's "Travels in Europe, Africa, and Asia between 1770 and 1779," London, 1793, 1 vol., and Dr. Sparrman's "Voyage to the Cape of Good Hope," 1786, vol. i. The official papers published from time to time by Parliament are likewise of great interest and importance.

† Parliamentary Papers relative to the Cape, published in 1835, p. 28.

Towards the latter part of the last century the Dutch colonists at the Cape became acquainted with a race of men quite distinct from the Hottentots and the Bosjesmans. These were the Caffres, or Kafirs, a nation which is supposed, with the greatest probability, to have migrated from the north-east parts of Africa about the fifteenth or sixteenth centuries, and which retains the rite of circumcision, the abhorrence of swine's flesh, and several other Jewish observances. These people inhabit a fine tract of country, situated north-east of the Great Fish River, and apparently comprehending within its original boundaries our present colony of Port Natal. Their territory originally extended much further westward, however, and was circumscribed by the gradual encroachments of the colonists at the Cape during the course of the eighteenth century.

The Cape authorities for long have been most anxious to prevent all intercourse taking place between their subjects and the Kafirs; but in process of time the "Boors," having become a class very powerful both in numbers and wealth, disregarded the proclamations issued from head-quarters at the Cape upon the subject, and, about the year 1770, commenced that border warfare between the native tribes and themselves which led to such disastrous results, and has continued, even to our own time, to interrupt the peace and prosperity of this magnificent colony.

In the year 1780 the first "commando" on the part of the governor and council of the Cape was undertaken against the Kafirs. The result of this expedition was that the Kafirs were driven beyond the Great Fish River, which was declared thenceforth to be the boundary of the Cape Colony. The only way in which the Kafirs could retaliate, on anything like equal terms, was adopted by them upon this. They could not meet their enemies in open fight because they had no fire-arms; but they adopted the mode of "guerilla" warfare, or harassing their foes by sudden predatory expeditions, whereby immense damage was done from time to time to the interests of the border inhabitants.

About this time the minds of men in every part of the world began to be agitated by the revolution of France, and the effects of that great moral convulsion were felt in an alarming degree in all classes of society at the colony of the Cape of Good Hope. Republican and socialistic views spread rapidly among the Dutch settlers, who, with the other descendants of Europeans, numbered at that time about 20,000 persons; and, as none but a few of the higher officials of the colony opposed the movement, a declaration of independence from the authorities of the Dutch East India Company appeared at one time almost imminent. The state of affairs in the colony was rendered all the more serious by the attitude of the negro slaves, who outnumbered their white masters in the proportion of about four to one, and who, having heard these individuals descant upon "Liberty and Equality" and the "Rights of Man," began to make some movement towards the assertion of these principles for themselves, and thus society appeared on the eve of total disorganisation.

At this serious crisis of affairs, an expedition sent out by Great Britain arrived most opportunely off the Cape (1795 A.D.). This armament had been nominally fitted out in the interest of the Prince of Orange, to secure to him the South African colony when Holland had banished him from her shores, and compelled him to take refuge in England. It was commanded by Sir James Craig, and comprehended an effective force both naval and military. On its arrival the governor called a council of war, in which it was determined by the majority of voices to resist the attack, and the regular troops, with a few hundred militia, were drawn out for the defence of the colony. After a few hours' contest, however, further resistance was deemed hopeless, and a flag of truce having been sent by the Dutch, a capitulation was speedily signed. The English took possession of Cape Town, and the greater part of the Dutch officials were allowed to retain their posts, those only being dismissed who had shown a sympathy with the democratic party.

Lord Macartney was sent out as governor of Cape Colony in the year 1797, and his administration was distinguished by various reformatory enactments. His secretary, Sir John Barrow, published in 1806 his travels in South Africa, which first conveyed to our countrymen generally an accurate idea of the condition of that vast country, and our newly acquired territory there. The number of Europeans in the various provinces of Cape Colony appears about that time to have been 20,000.

In 1803 the Peace of Amiens was concluded, according to the provisions of which the British government gave up Cape Colony once more to that of Holland, in whose name they had hitherto held that province. Many of the inhabitants appear to have submitted with great reluctance to a change which was to deprive them once more of English rule, under which lawlessness and violence of every kind had received a powerful and salutary check. The history of this second period of Dutch administration at the Cape is short, and generally speaking unimportant. The war between England and France was ere long renewed, and the British government, apprehending that the enemy would contrive to make the Cape of Good Hope a stepping-stone for their designs on our Indian empire, determined to prevent such a catastrophe by annexing the province in question to the possession of the British crown. Accordingly, an expedition was sent out under the command of Sir David Baird[*],

---

[*] Distinguished at the siege of Seringapatam in 1799.

which arrived off Table Bay on the 4th January, 1806. A slight resistance was made on the part of the Dutch military force, who were, however, defeated in an engagement with the English, and Sir David Baird advanced towards Cape Town with the intention of making an assault. Upon this the commandant, seeing that the inhabitants were by no means disposed for resistance, sent a flag of truce, and demanded terms of capitulation. These having been agreed upon, the British flag was soon seen waving once more from the castle of Cape Town, and the English fleet anchored within the bay. General Jansens, a brave and able commander, endeavoured for a few days to hold out the country against the British invaders, but was soon forced to come to terms, according to which he and his troops were transported to Holland in English vessels, on giving their " parole " not to serve against England or her allies until their arrival there.

CHAP. IV.

THE CAPE OF GOOD HOPE.—PORT NATAL.

THE occupation of Cape Colony was thus completed with little struggle or bloodshed by the British authorities, and has ever since remained in the undisturbed possession of that power. The principal adversaries with whom our government there have had to contend have been of a twofold nature; the Boors, or European inhabitants (chiefly Dutch), of the frontier provinces, a lawless and independent race, who have more than once risen in open insurrection against the authorities at the Cape, and by their predatory habits have contributed the most towards the continuance of hostile feelings on the part of the aboriginal tribes; and the Kafirs, with whom our troops have had several very severe encounters during the present century, but who, at last, have been brought, we may hope, to the condition of peaceful and profitable neighbours.

In the year 1808, the law was passed in England by which the slave-carrying trade was rendered illegal as far as this country and its colonies were concerned.

Several cargoes of negroes had been landed at the Cape, at its conquest by the British forces; the state of the slaves in that colony now, however, began to be ameliorated, and some progress was made towards the education of their children.

The Hottentot tribes upon the frontier of Cape Colony became about this time completely subject to the authority of Great Britain. This people proved very valuable servants and farm-labourers to the Europeans of the frontier districts, and it is only to be regretted that their rights, as a free nation and as British subjects, were not more strictly recognised at that time by the authorities of the colony.

The relations between the frontier Boors and the Kafir tribes of the Zuurveld district, that large territory lying on the right bank of the Great Fish River, had become very disturbed for some years past, until at length, in the years 1811-12, the government issued a commando, ordering the assemblage of the militia of the country, and at the same time proclaimed that all the Kafirs in the Zuurveld should migrate to the further bank of the Great Fish River. This was an act wholly unjustifiable, for the Kafir tribes, against whom it was urged, amounting to some 20,000, had in the course of years become more and more disposed towards civilisation from their intercourse with the Europeans, and many of them were settled down as domestics in the families of the latter. It is true that many depredations were committed by the wilder part of their community, and acts of violence had been frequent between them and the Boors; but in the former case, Parliament was assured on valuable testimony that restitution was always to be had by applying to the chiefs of the tribe to which the offender belonged*, while in the latter case, it is to be feared, that the guilt lay very often on the Boors themselves, who were but half civilised in their habits and manners, and of a very lawless disposition.

On the present occasion the chiefs Zlambie and Congo, as well as their subjects, made the most earnest entreaties against this unjust and impolitic sentence. All was in vain, however, a large force being marched to the frontier in three divisions under the command of Colonel Graham, to carry out the orders of the government. One very sad result ensued in the murder of Mr. Stockenstrom, the Landdrost of Uitenhage, one of the most distinguished men at that time possessed by the colony. This gentleman seeing a band of Kafir chiefs with their followers at no great distance, rode down among them almost without any attendants, relying on the respect and affection which had always attended him personally among that people, and with the benevolent intention of bringing matters to a peaceful issue in the present case. During the course of their interview, some suspicion of treachery arose

* Parliamentary Papers, 1835, part i. p. 174.

suddenly in the minds of the savages, and Mr. Stockenstrom, with the greater part of his suite, was murdered on the spot, a few only escaping to tell the tale.*

After their expulsion beyond the Fish River, the most severe penalties were inflicted on those Kafirs who were found upon the right bank, many of them being put to death. Heavy fines and punishments were also threatened against colonists who should be found on the left side of the river without a pass from the authorities; thus it was attempted to annihilate all intercourse between the two races.

About the year 1815, a strong system of military posts was established along the south-east frontier of the colony, the head-quarters being established at Graham's Town, which has since become a very flourishing settlement. At the same time the armed militia of the colony was disbanded, and a body of infantry was raised among the Hottentots, to be maintained by local taxation.

In the same year, 1815, an insurrection was attempted on the part of the Boors, that portion of the population which had from the first been most hostile to the British rule, as indeed they appear to have been to every other. They tried at first to gain over the Kafir chief Gaika to their assistance, by promising the

---

* Such was the view of this tragic event taken by Ensign Stockenstrom, afterwards Landdrost of Great Reynet. Some authors have endeavoured to prove it to have been an act of premeditated treachery.

restoration of the Zuurveld to his countrymen. That noble chief, however, in his reply pretty clearly intimated a suspicion of treachery on their part towards himself and his people, but at all events declined "to place himself, like a silly deer, between a lion" (the British power) "on the one side, and a wolf" (the Dutch Boors) "on the other." The insurgents were speedily forced to surrender.

At that time the governor of the colony was Lord Charles Somerset, whose false policy in treating with the Kafirs did much, it is to be feared, towards aggravating their relations towards our government. He persisted in recognising Gaika as the head of the entire nation, although that chieftain disclaimed any such high prerogative, and was, in fact, the inferior in rank of one of his brother chiefs.

In 1822 the unsettled state of affairs at the Cape caused a commission of inquiry to be despatched from England, whose researches into the local abuses and their causes led to several very valuable reforms. Among these perhaps the most important was the passing of the fiftieth ordinance, or "Magna Charta" of the Hottentot tribes under British influence, the chief provisions of which were, securing to them a footing of equality with all other British subjects, and permitting free access to them on the part of the missionaries and others whose object it might be to enlighten and instruct this benighted people.

In 1829 the authorities of the Cape further incensed the warlike Kafir nation by the expulsion of Macomo, one of their powerful chieftains, and his followers from the Kat River, in the neighbourhood of which they founded a Hottentot settlement.

In the month of December, 1834, a formidable invasion of the Kafirs took place on the frontier districts of the colony, which were ravaged for many miles, the men being slain and the cattle driven away, while on the other hand women and children were treated with marked gentleness. Great alarm was felt in Graham's Town, which was converted into a fortified camp for the time being. Sir Benjamin D'Urban, the governor-general, took vigorous measures for the safety of the border districts, and went himself thither to superintend the conduct of the war. The most striking episode of this contest, which, like all border wars, was of a very desultory character, and one which it is most difficult for a historian to detail, was the barbarous and most unjustifiable slaughter of the chieftain Hintza, while a hostage in the British camp. This sad event, in which it is to be regretted that Colonel, after Sir Harry Smith, took too prominent a part, was severely condemned by the local authorities at the time, and afterwards by the English government.

A treaty was signed in September 1835, by which the contest with the Kafirs was for the time appeased. According to the provisions of this treaty, the Kafir chiefs agreed to recognise the supreme authority of the British crown, under which they were to hold a kind of feudal tenure. These terms were not, however, approved of by the government or people of England, and at the command of the former, a good deal of the territory which had been seized from the Kafirs was restored to that people.

In 1834, the bill was passed by which slavery was abolished within the British dominions. At that time the number of slaves of every class, and of both sexes, including children under six years of age, in the South African colony was 35,751; they were of two races, partly negroes and partly Malays. In consequence of this measure, and from apprehension of being enrolled in a colonial militia, a great number of the Boors sold or threw up their farms, and migrated from Cape Colony, some in the direction of the Orange River, and others to Natal.

Sir Benjamin D'Urban was succeeded in 1838 by Sir George Grey, during whose six years' administration the colony remained at peace with the Kafirs. He was followed in 1844 by Sir Peregrine Maitland, who did not prove so successful in his policy towards these formidable neighbours, several of his measures towards them being of a very irritating character. In November 1847, Sir Harry Smith was appointed governor of Cape Colony, and at once entered upon a course of measures calculated to produce an open breach between himself and the Kafir nation. He seems to have lost no opportunity of insulting their greatest and most honoured chieftains; and upon one occasion, at an interview with Macomo, which he had himself requested, in return for that chieftain's cordial greeting, he collared him, and throwing him on the ground put his foot upon his neck. When he rose up, Macomo looked the old soldier quietly in the face, and said, "I always thought you a great man until this day."* The new governor, moreover, portioned out the Kafir territory, which he now affected to consider that of a conquered people, into territories bearing English titles, and sold lots of land therein to European settlers.

In the year 1849, great excitement was produced throughout the Cape territory by the home government sending out a ship load of convicts, with the intention of settling them on that colony. The opposition of the inhabitants to this measure was most urgent and unanimous, and the local government from the first saw the necessity of yielding to their request, and refusing permission to the convicts to land on the arrival of the Neptune, the vessel in which they had been conveyed. On hearing of these events, the imperial government sent an order to the Neptune to proceed to Van Diemen's Land, and the idea of con-

---

* Parliamentary Papers, August, 1851, p. 387.

verting the Cape into a penal settlement was wisely abandoned.

In 1850 a great excitement was observed among the Kafir tribes, and unmistakable signs of hostility between them and the European colonists increased. Sir. H. Smith took his departure for the frontier towards the end of that year, and there peremptorily called a conference of the Kafir chiefs. At the meeting, however, Sandilli, the most influential of all of them at that moment refused to present himself, alleging fear of treachery on the part of the English authorities. For this misdemeanor the governor solemnly took upon himself to depose Sandilli in the name of the sovereign of Great Britain, and named first an English officer, but afterwards with greater judgment, Sandilli's own mother, as vicegerent of that chieftain's tribe. At a second conference with the other chiefs, Sir H. Smith promised that he would not "send any red-coats to hunt Sandilli," though he proclaimed a reward of 500*l*. for his capture, and 250*l*. for that of his mother. Nevertheless, Sir Harry sent a body of 500 men under Colonel Mackinnon only four days afterwards in pursuit of the chief, and to hunt him out of his supposed place of concealment. At the close of the year Sir H. Smith was shut up in Fort Cox, with a small band of soldiers, where he was entirely surrounded by the Gaika Kafirs, who had deemed his last acts towards Sandilli as nothing less than a declaration of war against their nation. For some time great alarm was felt for the governor's safety, but he managed to escape on the last day of the year, under the guise of a rifleman, accompanied by a few Hottentots of that corps, and was so fortunate as to elude the pursuit of the Kafirs.

Shortly after the commencement of the new year (1851), a partial defection took place among the Hottentots of the Kat River settlement, in consequence of which it was thought necessary to break up that valuable community. Nevertheless, the confidence of our government in the Hottentot nation generally appears to have remained unshaken throughout this difficult contest.

During the year 1852, Sir H. Smith was superseded by Sir George Cathcart, as civil and military governor of Cape Colony. By this time, the Gaika tribe of Kafirs, with whom we were at war, were in a great measure dispersed and stripped of their resources. About the commencement of the following year, 1853, the war was brought to a conclusion by the voluntary submission of Sandilli, with whom, as the principal chief of the Gaikas, the governor concluded a treaty, the provisions of which seem to have laid heavily upon that nation, especially that having reference to the new lands assigned to them for a place of residence, and which Sandilli and his brother chieftains declared to be not large enough for their maintenance.

Since that period, the colony has enjoyed external tranquillity, and its resources have been multiplied within. A liberal constitution has been accorded to it by the home government, and there are not a few indications that it is hereafter destined to become one of the most illustrious offshoots of British enterprise and industry. At the census of 1849, the entire inhabitants of the colony were stated at 285,279; of these, some 90,000 are whites, and 190,000 coloured races.

SETTLEMENT OF NATAL.

The advantages likely to result from the establishment of a commercial station on the south-east coast of Africa were early noted by the Dutch governors at the Cape, and advances were made, even before the close of the seventeenth century, to purchase from the aborigines a portion of territory in the neighbourhood of Delagoa Bay. Nothing really effective in the matter was accomplished, however, until after the commencement of the present century. Since that period, several first efforts to found a colony in that direction have been made. The authorities at the Cape were more especially urged to this measure by the migration of the Boors towards Port Natal, 1835-6, as these personages, left to themselves, were evidently meditating to throw off British allegiance and erect themselves into an independent community. Small bodies of troops were sent therefore successively in 1838 and 1841, and the settlement of Port Natal taken possession of in the name of the sovereign of England. A flourishing town has since risen at D'Urban, Port Natal, and several large immigrations have taken place from the northern country of late years. The white population was estimated some years ago at 6000, the coloured at 115,000. The climate is described as delightful, and the temperature very moderate.

SECTION V.

REGIONS OF THE SOUTHERN OCEAN.

CHAPTER I.

AUSTRALIA: ITS DISCOVERY AND EARLY HISTORY.—COLONY OF NEW SOUTH WALES.

THIS immense territory is situated between 10° 45′ and 38° 45′ S. lat., and 112° 20′ and 153° 30′ E. long. of Greenwich. Its area is estimated at 2,690,810 square miles, while it has a coast line of 7750 miles in circumference. In relative size, as contrasted with the other great divisions of the earth, it stands to Asia in the proportion of 3 to 17, to America of 3 to 17, to Africa of 3 to 12, and to Europe of 3 to 4.

It is believed that the existence of Australia was known to the Chinese for many ages previous to the birth of modern history: but of this we appear to possess little direct evidence. Of its discovery by Europeans we have palpable proof very soon after the commencement of the 16th century, though it is not easy, perhaps, to settle which among the various national competitors can lay claim to distinction of its primitive discovery. Spain, Holland, France, England, and Portugal, all, nevertheless, contributed their fragment to the general amount of information on the subject. With the progress of the seventeenth and eighteenth centuries, the knowledge of Europeans with reference to Australia, or New Holland, continued to extend itself until the expeditions of Captain Cook, a man whose public and private virtues will render his name celebrated to unborn generations. This great voyager proved beyond dispute the insularity of this vast southern land; and by his surveys of its eastern coast, on which he bestowed the name of New South Wales, led to the settlement of that territory as a penal colony of Great Britain.

Of the aspect of this vast region it is very difficult to give any direct account, for but a small portion of it has hitherto been trodden by the foot of civilised man. Some describe the interior as consisting of an immense plain, sometimes densely covered with vegetation, and at others stretching out into interminable deserts of sand and stone. Captain Sturt, who set out from Adelaide in 1845 on a journey of discovery into the interior, describes it, as far as lat. 25° and long. E. 138°, as consisting of sand ridges, perfectly insurmountable, and close to one another, the whole aspect of the country being nothing but sand. In this account he is borne out by the general evidence of all who have penetrated into these inhospitable regions. But yet we are assured by one who has good opportunities of testing the truth of his assertions, that making large allowances for the barren central region, and for the sandstone wastes in other places, there probably is not less than two million square miles capable of yielding in abundance the productions of the temperate and of the torrid zones, and where horned cattle and sheep may be multiplied to an extent that would furnish all the inhabitants of Europe with animal food.*

NEW SOUTH WALES.

The history of this important colony is so closely connected with that of the transportation of convicts by the British government, that it will be necessary to say a few preliminary words on the latter subject before we proceed with our narrative.

Transportation was first resorted to in the reign of Elizabeth, having been rendered necessary by the great increase of crime and pauperism which were entailed by the abolition of monasteries in the reign of her father Henry VIII. During the seventeenth and eighteenth centuries the practice of transporting criminals to the American colonies prevailed for a time to a considerable extent. The numbers trans-

* Montgomery Martin on the Colonies — Australia, b. i. ch. i. p. 401.

ported latterly appear to have amounted to some 2000 annually, and these poor creatures were there subjected to the treatment of slaves, being in fact sold for about 20*l*. a-head.

On the severance of America from this country, the practice of transporting criminals to her shores was of course no longer feasible, and it became a grave question at home to what country it would thenceforth be possible to transmit them. It was about that period that Captain Cook had interested and favourably impressed the general mind by his description of New South Wales, and it was accordingly determined at the close of the year 1786 to transport a fleet of convicts to the neighbourhood of Botany Bay, on the coast of that newly-discovered region.

This first effort towards the settlement of that mighty region consisted of 565 male and 192 female convicts, who were conveyed in six transport vessels, attended by three store-ships, and guarded by two armed vessels, the whole convoy being under the command of Captain Arthur Phillip, R.N. The place of settlement was ultimately fixed on the site of the present City of Sydney, the capital of New South Wales; and here for several years great misery and hardship seems to have been the lot of the infant colony. These arose in part from the loss of vessels which had been sent from home laden with provisions for the colony, and in part from the thick influx of new gangs of convicts, by which great confusion was introduced into its affairs, and the governor and other principal functionaries found their task a very heavy one. Captain Phillip quitted New South Wales in 1792, having presided over the administration for several years with great credit, and his departure was much lamented. His next successor was Governor Hunter, and Governor Bligh, the latter of whom had been formerly notorious for his treatment of the mutineers of the Bounty. This last dignitary made himself so unpopular in New South Wales, that the population rose as one man at last and deposed him. This occurred on the 26th January, 1808. The next governor was General Lachlan Macquarie. His administration continued during twelve years, and was signalised by many acts of a very beneficial nature to the colony. He did much to raise the character and condition of the convict part of the population. Some, however, thought that he carried his regard for them too far, and the result was a spirit of party hostility for some years between the free and the convict portions of the community in New South Wales. Sir Thomas Brisbane succeeded Major-General Macquarie in 1821, and was in his turn succeeded by Sir Ralph Darling, who, being a military man and a stern disciplinarian, was thought by many to have exercised unreasonable severity during his term of office. In the year 1848 a step was taken towards making New South Wales a constitutional colony, and it has since that period been increasing in wealth and general prosperity, though it has experienced some severe checks of a temporary nature, arising either from causes of a natural order, as droughts, or from an unreasonable spirit of speculation among the inhabitants of the colony, by an order in council issued in 1848, which decreed that the transportation of convicts to that settlement should cease "from and after the 1st August, 1848." The government of New South Wales was for many years after its foundation of a very despotic character, being entirely in the hands of the governor for the time being, with a few assistant judges and councillors, mostly military and naval officers. The great distance of the settlement from Great Britain made all appeal on the part of the inhabitants to the home government a very arduous and expensive course. In 1823–4 a supreme council was appointed to assist the governor, who should consist of the commanding officer of the troops, the archdeacon, the colonial secretary, the treasurer, and the attorney-general. In 1842 a legislative council, to consist of thirty-six members, was decreed for the colony. Of these one-third was nominated by the Crown, and the other two-thirds elected by the suffrage of the people, the franchise extending to freeholders of property to the value of 200*l.*, or to householders occupying a house of the yearly value of 20*l.* In 1849 a committee of privy council made a report to the

Crown on the subject of colonial self-government, in reference to our Australian colonies. The question was then much agitated as to the expediency of one or two legislative chambers in our distant settlements, and the committee recommended that the plan already adopted in New South Wales of a single legislative chamber, of which one-third should be nominated by the Crown, and the other two-thirds by popular suffrage, should be continued there and extended to the other Australian colonies. At the same time the committee stated their opinion that ancient precedent in all our older settlements was decidedly in favour of two separate chambers, one nominated by the Crown, and the other by the people; and they further alleged that they only recommended the adoption of a different line of action in the present case as a temporary expedient. A bill was accordingly passed through Parliament in the session of 1850, in which the suggestion of the committee as to a single legislative chamber for each of our Australian colonies was carried out, while full liberty was accorded to each colony, subject to the approval of the Crown, to make any change in the constitution then provided for them.

Another enactment of this bill provided for a general assembly of the Australian colonies, to be held under the auspices of a governor-general* of

---

* The governor-general was to be nominated by the home government of the different Australian colonies.

Australia, and the members of which were to be nominated by the legislatures of the various provinces, according to the relative population of each. This body was to legislate upon all matters bearing upon the general interests of the Australian colonies.

This same bill, moreover, enacted that Port Phillip should be separated from New South Wales, and erected into a separate colony under the name of Victoria.

In the year 1850, the population of this great and flourishing colony amounted to 250,000 inhabitants, a surprising result when we consider its recent foundation, and that as a penal settlement and under many discouraging auspices. The expenditure of New South Wales while it contained a convict establishment was a heavy drain on the imperial exchequer, 8,483,519*l*. having been expended for this purpose on the two provinces of New South Wales and Van Diemen's Land, from the year 1786, when a cargo of convicts was first landed in the former country, down to the year 1837.* Reliable statements prove, nevertheless, that this mode of punishment by transportation, would be not only humane, but economical, as compared with other methods of treating the class of malefactors; not to mention its beneficial effects in the formation of new settlements beyond the seas, and the impulse accorded by it to the employment of useful labour in those

---

*. Report of Committee of the Commons, 1837–8, on Transportation. See M. Martin, 19, p. 564.

already founded. The colony has been on the whole, in a state of great prosperity of late years; its pastoral* resources have already been indisputably developed, and great results are hereafter to be hoped for from the opening out of its agricultural and mineral wealth, together with its fisheries and its commercial capabilities generally.

* In 1850, the colony contained 12,000,000 sheep, 2,000,000 horned cattle, 150,000 horses, 100,000 pigs.

CHAP. II.

HISTORY OF VICTORIA, SOUTH AUSTRALIA AND WEST AUSTRALIA.

PORT PHILLIP, or Victoria, as it has now been decreed to be named, in honour of the reigning sovereign, occupies the portion of this vast territory of Australia which lies upon the extreme south-east coast, and contains an area of some 97,000 square miles. It has furthermore been designated by the term Australia Felix, from the richness of its soil and the beauty of its scenery. The illustrious Captain Cook was one of the first, if not the very first, to visit the southern shores of Australia in the year 1770. In 1798, Mr. Bass entered the straits named after him in a whale-boat with a few seamen, and towards the close of the same year these straits were passed through, and the whole notion of Van Diemen's Land being merely a peninsula thus finally exploded.

It appears to have been from a fear of the French obtaining the territory for their own purposes, that our government was induced, in 1804, to send out a convoy of convicts to the neighbourhood of Port

Phillip. This expedition resulted unsuccessfully, and Colonel Collins, the commander-in-chief, ultimately removed to Van Diemen's Land, where he founded the colony of Hobart Town. For twenty years this fine portion of Australia now remained a blank, until in 1824 it was visited by two English travellers from New South Wales, who published a flattering description of the country along the south coast, which drew attention to that point forthwith, and in 1826, Western Point was formally taken possession of in the name of the Crown, and a small fort erected on Phillip Island at the mouth of the harbour. For some years the British government used all their efforts to check the progress of colonisation on the southern coast of this great continent, and in consequence of their senseless objections made on these points, the bargains concluded with the natives for large tracts of territory by several private individuals, and companies did not at that time receive the sanction of the Crown. Nevertheless, the settlements in the neighbourhood of Port Phillip and Western Point continued to thrive, and the foundations were laid at that time of the now flourishing city of Melbourne.

In 1836 the government sent a gentleman to preside over the newly formed society in this quarter of the world, and at the same time it was proclaimed by order of Sir Richard Bourke, the governor of that colony, that no purchases of land made with the chiefs of native tribes by individuals or private companies could be lawfully ratified by the Crown, this seems to have been afterwards the opinion of the highest legal authorities both in Australia and Great Britain. Meanwhile the new settlement continued to expand beyond all former experience. In 1836, within one year of its original formation, 30,000 sheep had arrived from Van Diemen's Land. Mr. Stewart, the magistrate despatched from New South Wales, reported to his superiors that 177 persons had settled in the neighbourhood of Port Phillip, bringing with them property to the amount of 100,000*l.* In consequence of the judgment pronounced by the great legal authorities, both at home and in the colonies, the Van Diemen's Land Association and other private companies formed for the colonisation of this hopeful region came to an abrupt close; they had nevertheless a remission of 7000*l.* made them by government of the purchase money of any lands they might purchase in Australia Felix; this was in consideration of their previous payments to the native tribes. In 1836, Sir Thomas Mitchell, surveyor-general of the colony, made an overland journey from New South Wales to the neighbourhood of Port Phillip, and was so struck with the beauty and fertility of this part of the country that he gave it the appellation of Australia Felix.

The extraordinary prosperity which this settlement has since enjoyed, is too recent to claim any lengthened description in a work of this nature. Port Phillip is now an independent colony, under the illustrious name of Victoria, and with a population of many thousands who have hurried thither from all parts of the world, attracted by the marvels of her gold "diggings." This rapid growth has not been without serious checks of a commercial or financial character. But a few years back the insolvencies are said to have been almost universal among the settlers; it is now recovering from a severe crisis in its affairs, and we trust has a long and prosperous career in view for the future.

The population of Victoria, was, in 1851, 95,000; in the following year (1852), it had amounted to 200,000—a rise without any precedent in the world's history. The shipping inwards in the former year was 126,000 tons, in the latter it was 408,000 tons. The revenue in 1851, was 380,000*l.*; in 1852 it was 1,577,000*l.*—342,000*l.* being raised from custom duties. In 1851, the value of imports was 1,056,000*l.*; in 1852 it was 4,044,000*l.* The exports of the former year were 1,424,000; of the latter, 7,452,000*l.* The population of Melbourne increased from 23,000 in 1851, to 80,000 in 1852; that of Geelong in the same period from 8000 to 20,000.

SOUTH AUSTRALIA.

The colony of South Australia is situated about the centre of the southern coast of that vast territory, and to the west of New South Wales and Victoria, the latter of which colonies it borders south of the River Murray. Its area is estimated at not less than 300,000 square miles, but of this the greater part has been as yet very imperfectly explored; its scenery is described as being, in parts, very picturesque and beautiful.

Public attention was first roused towards this portion of Australian territory by the discoveries of Oxley and Cunningham in the interior, between the years 1817-28; but to Captain Sturt and his celebrated " exploring expedition" in 1830, appears due the greatest merit in laying open this vast region to his countrymen. The Governor of New South Wales, Sir Ralph Darling, followed the advice given him by this gentleman on his return to Sydney, and sent another expedition in April, 1831, under Captain Barber and Mr. Kent, to the Gulf of St. Vincent. The former gentleman was killed by the natives, in the neighbourhood of Lake Victoria. Mr. Kent on his return fully corroborated the statement of Captain Sturt, pronouncing it an admirable region whereon to found a new settlement. In consequence of this, a committee of gentlemen was formed in London in the course of the year 1831, to consider the means of promoting colonisation in South Australia. It is to be regretted that the principal promoters of this excellent undertaking marred their success by their controversies on the subject of the sale of the crown-lands in our colonies. The unreasonably high prices which have been assigned to these by some of the highest authorities in our colonies, have checked the progress of emigration within our territories very much of late years, and have given a great impetus to emigration from the United Kingdom to the United States territories, where a very opposite plan has been pursued, immense tracts of waste land having been surveyed by the government and then laid out in lots at the very small charge of about two shillings per acre, whereas, our colonial authorities at one time seem to have decided that twenty shillings per acre should be the minimum price of every kind of land, good, bad, or indifferent. Of late years the government of the United States are said to have advanced so far in the career of liberality as to have determined on giving away a small portion of land, entirely free of charge, to every immigrant who can give a voucher of respectability. On the other hand, much has been said of the unwholesome character, in many cases, of the land thus sold at nominal prices, or given away, and which we are told has proved a rapid grave to many an English, Scotch, and Irish emigrant. This, if true, ought only to prove an additional stimulus to our government to promote the sale of land at a low price among its subjects to our own colonies, where it is to be hoped their welfare in all respects will be better attended to.

In August, 1834, a bill was introduced into Parliament, under the sanction of the Duke of Wellington, and passed, for the formation of South Australia; the boundaries of the new province to be between 132° and 141° E. long. and the Southern Ocean and 26° of S. lat. with the adjacent islands. The new colony was not to be a penal one; when the population amounted to 50,000, a constitutional government was to be accorded to it. The price of land was originally fixed at twelve shillings per acre, but in the ensuing year, 1835, the commissioners for the colony, with Colonel Torrens for their chairman, raised it to the high amount of one pound per acre. This was soon found to be too high a price for any practical purposes, and it was once more reduced to about twelve shillings per acre, purchasers being allowed to receive for 81*l.*, one acre of town land, and 134 acres of country land, which was considered a fair bargain.

Nevertheless, it seems probable that the necessary sum for the foundation of the colony of South Australia, would not at that time have been raised by the sale of land lots, had not a few enterprising individuals come forward, under whose auspices was formed the South Australian Company, which bought 13,770 acres from the commissioners, which they sold at twelve shillings per acre, or leased on convenient terms.

At length, matters being in a sufficiently advanced state, the governor, Captain Hindmarsh, and other principal officials were appointed to the new settlement, and on the 20th March, 1836, the Cygnet was despatched from the metropolis, followed soon after by several other vessels conveying the first freights, both of men and goods, to these distant shores. The first landing place was Nepean Bay, in Kangaroo Island; Colonel Light, as surveyor-general, proceeded to examine the main coast round St. Vincent's Gulf, and ere long fixed upon a spot for the principal town; his judgment proved correct, for on that spot has since risen the thriving city of Adelaide. In the month of August, 1839, 7412 emigrants had arrived in the new colony, and 250,320 acres of land had been sold which produced 229,756*l.*; many of the purchasers of land had not, however, received as yet any returns for their outlay, and the condition of the new settlement was not considered, in many respects, to be satisfactory. There were as yet only 2500 acres in process of cultivation, and the colonial authorities were expending extravagant sums on public buildings and works of various kinds. To so great a height did this extravagance proceed under the second governor, Lieut.-Colonel Gawler, that only for four years after the commencement of the colony, the expenditure had risen to 140,000*l.* per annum, while the annual revenue did not as yet exceed 20,000*l.*; and extraordinary sums were laid out upon public works, some of which proved very futile in their result. At length, to use the language of Lord Stanley, the "bubble burst," the colonial bills were dishonoured, and Colonel Gawler was recalled by the home government. Great misery resulted, nevertheless, in the end to many unfortunate emigrants from these wild proceedings on the part of the authorities during the first four years or so of their career. Another great source of evil to the colony in its infantile state was the clumsy manner in which the authority of the principal officers was made to jostle, and which proved the source of infinite heart-burnings and quarrels, to the great draw-back of the prosperity of the new community.

In 1841, Captain Grey was appointed to succeed Colonel Gawler in the government of South Australia. Under the assiduous exertions of this public-spirited man, the colony ere long began to rise out of its severe difficulties, the expenses being retrenched in the course of one year (from 1841 to 1842) from 78,787*l.* to 19,173*l,* and every encouragement being held out to the emigrants to induce them to quit the town, and betake themselves to agricultural and pastoral employments. It is possible, however, that the progress of the settlement would have been very tardy had not discoveries of a wholly unlooked-for nature occurred in the shape of copper, lead, and silver mines. The first specimens were picked up quite accidentally in 1842-3 by Mr. Dutton and a son of Captain Bagot; and these two gentlemen combined to buy the land of which so much mineral wealth appeared to lie ready for the first claimant. This land, containing the copper mines of Kapunda, which they bought (eighty acres) for 80*l.*, they refused to sell some time after in London for 27,000*l.* The stimulus thus afforded to enterprise of every description has been developed with even increasing ardour. In 1857 the population of South Australia had risen to 109,917 persons. The revenue of the colony, which in 1840 amounted to only 30,000*l.*, in 1857 had increased to 726,326*l.* In 1857 the exports of the colony amounted to 1,744,180*l.*, while the imports amounted to 1,623,052*l.* This was a most satisfactory change from the state of things in 1840, when the value of the imports immensely exceeded that of the exports, by which means the colony was left sadly in debt to England and other countries. In 1857 the land under cultivation amounted to 235,965 acres, employing more than 10,000 persons. Altogether South Australia may now be considered one of the most flourishing possessions of the British crown.

WEST AUSTRALIA.

This extensive country, almost better known by the name of Swan River Settlement, occupies the whole western side of the Australian continent, from the 129th degree of east longitude, and comprises an area of 1,000,000 square miles, more than eight times the extent of the United Kingdom.

This portion of Australia was discovered in 1697 by Vlaming, a Dutch navigator, who gave the name of Swan River to the noble stream which flows through it, from the number of black swans he discerned on its banks. It was subsequently visited in 1801 by a French corvette, the officers of which explored the course of the river some way inland. In 1829 Captain Stirling directed the attention of the English government and people to the importance of our taking speedy possession of this vast territory, which it was then announced that our neighbours the French had thoughts of making a settlement. Accordingly the British flag was hoisted in 1829 near the entrance of Swan River, and the territory was taken formal possession of in the name of the British sovereign.

The government at home appeared very loth at that time to undertake the formation of a new settlement. Accordingly, some public-spirited individuals, at the head of whom were Mr. Thomas Peel and Sir Francis Vincent, offered to raise a sum of money for the conveyance of 10,000 British subjects to the neighbourhood of the Swan River, where they were to be provided with land at the smallest possible cost, which property might, however, after a certain term of years be reclaimed by the Crown, if it was found that the possessors in the interval had not laid a certain amount of it under cultivation.

By the noble exertions of these public-minded men — Mr. Peel, Colonel Latour, and others — various freights of emigrants and goods, including live stock of various kinds, were conveyed to the neighbourhood of Swan River during the years 1829-30-31. In the first year twenty-five vessels reached the new settlement; in the second, thirty; in the last, seventeen. So little preparation had been made beforehand for this large influx of persons that an endless amount of public and individual distress was the final result of an expedition without doubt rashly put into execution in the first instance. No public anchorage for ships had been secured previously, and in consequence not a few of the vessels were dashed to pieces on the beach. The detachment of settlers and goods arrived in the month of June, the middle of the winter in those regions. They found no sheds to shelter them from the pouring rain, and the miscellaneous crowd were huddled together on the beach, while bodies of armed and hostile natives watched them from a short distance. The consequence of these things was, that many persons gave themselves up to feelings of despair, and many more rushed to the spirit-casks to find consolation in the temporary oblivion of their misfortunes. Another circumstance which seems to have obstructed the progress of colonisation in Western Australia was the vast inequality in the terms on which the distribution of land was effected, not a little favouritism being shown, not only to the civil servants of the colony and officers of the army and navy, but even to many private persons, with no apparent claim on the consideration of the government. On the other hand, Mr. Thomas Peel, and several others among the early founders of the colony, were either ruined by their liberality, or at least have suffered a most disgraceful neglect of their just claims on the part of the government. Captain (afterwards Sir James) Stirling arrived at the mouth of Swan River, with several other (government) officers designated to high posts in the new-born colony on June 1st, 1829, and on the 17th of the same month his appointment as governor was announced by public proclamation. This gentleman received not less than 100,000 acres of land as his own private portion.

The distance of the Swan River settlement from Sydney being 1134 miles, no overland communication was then possible between the two places, and thus no cattle and live stock could be conveyed by that mode of transit to West Australia, as had been the case at an early period of the settlement of Port Phillip and Adelaide. The expense of conveying live stock by a long and dangerous sea voyage was, therefore, very great, every sheep being computed to cost the colonists 20*l*.; and when we consider the immense damage done to animals from the recklessness with which the early proceedings at the settlement were conducted, we may arrive at some idea of the destitution to which the emigrants were at that time reduced.

These disasters were modified by time, however, and the exertions of the more active and upright members of the infant community, and West Australia began slowly to raise itself to a condition of ease and plenty, though not of opulence. The Western Australian Association, for the promotion of that much neglected colony, was formed in London during the year 1835. It attempted to found a new settlement at Australind, near Leschenault Bay, in the county of Wellington, a plan which did not prove very successful in its results. For several years emigration to this noble colony ceased almost or entirely. It is only of late that it has begun to exhibit signs of greater prosperity. Meanwhile, we are assured by those who have had opportunity of judging, that among its little community crime is almost unknown, and that its present, who are in general its original settlers, have, in proportion to their numbers, effected a creditable extent of tillage, and evinced a very praiseworthy spirit.* A very active trade is beginning to spring up between West Australia and the Mauritius and Singapore. The chief export of the country, which consists in great measure of downs, and therefore invites to pastoral pursuits, is wool. The population a few years ago was 7000, a very slow rate of increase compared with the neighbouring colonies of South Australia and Victoria.

* M. Martin, vol. xxiv. p. 714.

CHAP. III.

TASMANIA.—ITS HISTORY AND STATISTICS.

VAN DIEMEN'S ISLAND, or as it is now generally called Tasmania, is a fine island lying to the south-east extremity of Australia, from which it is separated by a channel of about 100 miles in breadth called Bass' Straits. Its greatest length is about 230 miles; its greatest breadth nearly 200 miles; the area comprises nearly 24,000 square miles.

This island was discovered in the year 1642, by a Dutch navigator named Abel Jansz Tasman, and by him termed Van Diemen's Land, in honour of the governor-general of the Dutch East Indies. Tasman, however, believed it to be a peninsula, adhering by a neck of land to the larger country in the north. For more than a century after this the island of Van Diemen was unvisited by any European, until our own illustrious countryman, Captain James Cook, in 1769 sighted a portion of its coast. From that time the investigation of its real shape and character became a point of great interest with European navigators; but it was not until the years 1797–8 that Mr. Bass, the enterprising surgeon of H. M. S. "Reliance," obtained from the governor of New South Wales the necessary equipments for two expeditions, during which (both times in small and frail vessels), amid multiplied dangers, he achieved the entire navigation of the land, thus determining the point of its insularity. On the return of Mr. Bass and his colleague, Lieutenant Flinders, from the second of these two heroic expeditions, they gave such a promising description of the country, as far as they had been able to explore it, that Colonel King, Governor of the New South Wales colony, determined to form a settlement there, the more so, that it was rumoured at the time that the French had designs upon the island. The first settlement was made in 1803, by Lieutenant Bowen, who was despatched from Sydney with some convicts and a guard of soldiers. They landed at Risdon or Restdown Cove, and commenced building and clearing land. In May, 1804, they were attacked by some hundreds of the natives whom they repulsed with considerable slaughter. Soon after Lieutenant-Colonel Collins arrived from England with 400 convicts under his charge, guarded by fifty marines, and accompanied by several persons prepared to take high situations in the government of the colony. Colonel Collins having been invested with supreme authority in the new settlement, removed its position from

Risdon to Sullivan's Cove, and there laid the foundation of the noble city Hobarton. At this early period the settlers of all classes suffered great privations from the entirely new food they were compelled to take.

In 1804, another settlement was established on the Tamar, in the north part of the island, under Colonel Paterson. At first the scarcity was very great here also; but these little remnants were never quite forgotten by their brethren of New South Wales, who from time to time sent them cargoes of supplies. In 1813, Van Diemen's Land became somewhat of a free colony, having been previously a strictly penal settlement; merchant vessels were allowed to enter and trade in her ports; in 1816 the island commenced exporting grain to her mother colony of New South Wales; and in 1819 free emigrants were permitted to settle in her. About this time commenced the fearful practice of bushranging, which was conducted here principally by runaway convicts. As in the history of other infant settlements, it ere long attained a barbarous notoriety, and is even said to have been attended by cannibalism in a few extreme cases. Lieutenant Sorell was appointed governor of Van Diemen's Land in 1817; his term of office closed in 1824. We are assured he found the island a wilderness, and left it possessed of commerce, buildings, roads, and bridges, a number of wealthy emigrants, and the inhabitants wearing the appearance of prosperity.* His successor, however, found that speculation had been advancing at a great rate, in consequence of which there was something of a mercantile re-action to be met and ameliorated. The ravages of the gangs of bushrangers still, and for some years afterwards, continued to hold the peaceful and orderly part of the community in alarm; they have long since, however, ceased to be any more than a traditional name in the island. The aborigines of Van Diemen's Land have been described as a very interesting race of men in many respects, but even less "susceptible of intellectual cultivation, and the most obnoxious to civilisation in any form."† This unfortunate nation has met with a fate similar to that of so many of their savage brethren in other countries and climes, having been gradually attenuated in numbers and strength for a course of years, and at last, when it would have been an act of cruelty to allow them to remain in their weakened condition, a prey to the bushranger and other lawless members of the white community, being shipped off to Flinder's Island (at the entrance of Bass' Straits). They were subsequently removed to Maria Island, on the south-east coast of Tasmania, and in 1848 there remained twelve men, twenty-three women, and one male child, of pure native blood.

In the month of December, 1825, orders arrived

* Van Diemen's Land, by Henry Melville. Hobart Town, 1832.
† M. Martin.

from home, whereby Van Diemen's Land was elevated to the rank of an independent colony, and was declared to form a distinct government from New South Wales. At that time the governorship was in the hands of Lieutenant-Colonel Arthur, to whose able and considerate management of affairs during the twelve years of his rule, the colony is indebted for many improvements and a considerable enlargement of its prosperity. Among other excellent reforms during his administration, was the entire subversion of a monetary system which had been long prevalent in the island, and being conducted on false principles had led to great confusion in the currency.

In 1830, the inhabitants of Tasmania began ardently to desire an elective legislature, and petitioned the imperial government on this important subject. Governor Arthur appears to have coincided with their aspirations on this point, and to have seconded them in his despatches to the colonial office in London. The request for constitutional government was not, however, at that time granted to the colony. In 1836 closed the administration of Colonel Arthur, who was succeeded by Sir John Franklin, that hero of Arctic discovery, whose loss this nation and the whole civilised world still deplores. During his administration the restrictive law was passed, whereby land was raised to a high minimum price per acre. The effect of this enactment was not less disastrous here than it proved in the other Australian colonies, and Sir J. Franklin informed Lord Stanley, the Colonial Secretary at the time, that "your Lordship will perceive that this instruction is in effect an instruction virtually abolishing sales of land in Van Diemen's Land, and must accordingly put an end to the already declining land sales."

After the year 1840, when transportation to New South Wales was made to cease, Van Diemen's Land became for some years the greatest, indeed, almost the only convict settlement in the British empire; and very distressing consequences followed with regard to the moral character of its population. Petitions were sent to the Imperial Parliament, and to the Throne, in 1845, 1848 and 1849, which obtained the signatures of by far the greater part of the respectable population of the island, praying that this great evil might be removed from their shores. These documents give a very gratifying account of the progress made by the colony. A few data will here enlighten the reader somewhat on this question. The population of the island, which was in 1824, 12,700 souls, had increased in 1840 to above 40,000; in 1848, it amounted to 74,741. The number of acres in cultivation advanced between the years 1824-40, from 25,000 to 124,000; the colonial shipping, from one vessel to 141 vessels, comprising 12,491 tons; the imports from 62,000*l.* to 988,356*l.*; the exports from 14,500*l.*, to 867,007*l.*; the colonial fixed revenue from 16,863*l.* to 118,541*l.*

The transportation of convicts to Van Diemen's Land has entirely ceased now for several years, and the best hopes cannot fail to be expressed as to the future of a country so happily situated, and possessed of many natural charms.

CHAP. IV.

NEW ZEALAND. — GEOGRAPHICAL ACCOUNT AND HISTORY.

This interesting country, situated almost at the antipodes of our own, has for long formed a subject of dispute among European nations, as to which of them could claim the honour of its first discovery, the French assigning it to De Gonville, the Spanish to Juan Fenandez. The first navigator from whom we have any specific accounts of the country, is Tasman, who visited its shores during the progress of his famous voyage of discovery, which he undertook in the year 1642, under the direction of the East India Company. From that period it is uncertain whether New Zealand was visited by any European vessel for more than a century, until the first voyage of our illustrious countryman, Captain Cook, in 1769. During this long interval, the prevalent notion among geographers was, that New Zealand was a part of the "Terra Australis," or great southern continent, about whose existence much futile discussion has been at various times expended.

Cook paid several visits to New Zealand, and has

recorded many particulars of interest with reference to the inhabitants whom he found there. The French Captain de Surville visited the island almost simultaneously with himself, in 1769, and New Zealand soon became the favourite point of exploration for European navigators; before long its insularity was demonstrated, and thus the notion exploded of a large continent existing in that part of the globe.

The aborigines of this country appear to be a fine race of men upon the whole, but fierce and sanguinary, and in their primitive condition, apparently addicted to cannibalism. During his second visit, in 1773, Captain Cook remarks of them:—"Their behaviour to us was manly and mild, showing on all occasions a readiness to oblige. They have some arts among them which they execute with judgment and unwearied patience; they are far less addicted to thieving than the other islanders of the South Seas, and I believe those in the same tribe, or such as are at peace with one another, are strictly honest among themselves."

Shortly after the formation of the convict settlement in New South Wales, intercourse began to spring up between that country and New Zealand, which was visited for its whale and seal fisheries. It is probable that the Europeans were not always straightforward and just in their dealings with the poor savages, who sometimes retaliated with dreadful ferocity, as in the case of the "Boyd" in 1809, which was destroyed by them, and its crew, with the exception of four individuals, massacred.

During the early years of the present century, the idea began to be entertained by several persons in England and New South Wales of establishing a mission in New Zealand, with a view of instructing its inhabitants in the precepts of the Christian religion. This design was embraced with great zeal by Mr. Marsden, senior chaplain of New South Wales; and the result of his endeavours there and in England was that a party of missionaries was sent out in 1814 to that country. At the same time Mr. Kendall (one of the missionaries) was empowered by the governor of New South Wales to act as magistrate in this distant country, with whose internal affairs England had no right whatever to meddle; and this, contemporary accounts inform us, was the commencement of British authority in New Zealand. How far English interference there has been for the benefit of the poor natives, it will be the business of this narrative hereafter to explain.

Mr. Marsden and his friends took up their position at the Bay of Islands, and, on the whole, made headway with the natives satisfactorily. A log church was soon erected, and we are informed that the savages showed great reverence during the celebration of service. These gentlemen were sent by the Church Missionary Society; but a few years subsequently, a

Wesleyan mission was established first at Wangaroa in 1822, and after a repulse thence, at the Hokianga river on the opposite shore of the north island. The two missions appear to have worked in harmony together; and a traveller, Mr. Jameson, attributes to their influence "the abolition of infanticide, polygamy, and the atrocities of native warfare, which have disappeared before the dawn of Christianity."* Soon after the establishment of the first missionaries in New Zealand, a desire arose among the mercantile body in New South Wales to establish a company for the purposes of trade with that country. Their desire was granted by Governor Macquarie, and a trade was opened at several parts of the coast, whale-oil, flax, timber, pork, and potatoes being exchanged by the inhabitants for fire-arms, blankets, axes, &c. &c.

The influence of the European sailors and others who from time to time landed from the trading vessels, is described as often very demoralising on the poor savages. A perfect community of runaway convicts, sailors, and other abandoned persons was at length established on the island; and these, we are told, obtained from the inhabitants the name of the "devil's missionaries."

In the year 1831 an address to the King of England was signed by thirteen chiefs of New Zealand, asking that monarch's protection against the outrageous con-

* Travels in New Zealand, by R. G. Jameson, Esq. p. 266.

duct of many of his subjects. In reply to this address Mr. J. Busby was sent from New South Wales, in 1832, in the character of "Resident" by the British government. The authority with which this new official was clothed proved, however, to be merely nominal, all cases of any importance which might be brought under his cognizance being directed to be transmitted to the supreme court at Sydney for trial. One of the first acts of the resident on his arrival in the country, was to suggest the adoption of a national flag by the New Zealanders, which was done with the approval of the government at home.

In 1835 the small community in New Zealand, —which, including both natives and Europeans, can hardly have surpassed 200,000 — was violently disturbed by the irregular proceedings of a vain Frenchman, the Baron de Thierry, who styled himself sovereign chief of that country, and called upon all others to give way before him. Mr. Busby deemed it necessary to take precautions against this formidable individual, fearing lest the French government had some hostile design latent under all this pomposity of an individual. That gentleman consequently induced the chiefs of the northern part of New Zealand to sign together a declaration of independence on the 28th of October, 1835, in which they "declare the independence of the country which is hereby constituted and declared to be an independent state, under the designation of the

United Tribes of New Zealand." It was agreed at the same time to send a copy of this declaration to his Majesty the King of England, to thank him for his acknowledgment of their flag; and, in return for the friendship and protection they have shown and are prepared to show to such of his subjects as have settled in their country, or resorted to its shores for the purposes of trade, they entreat that he will continue to be the parent of their infant state, and that he will become its protector from all attempts upon its independence.

European, and particularly British settlers, continued to arrive from time to time in New Zealand, although no regular plan of colonisation had as yet been thought of for that fine country. In 1838, Lord Normanby declares in a despatch that "a body of not less than 2000 British subjects had become permanent inhabitants of New Zealand." In 1836-7, a parliamentary committee sat on the subject of the aboriginal races of the British colonies, among others, those of New Zealand. The report ultimately issued by this committee contains much interesting matter, and concludes with some very severe remarks on the conduct of British subjects towards the native tribes.

About this time a "fever" for buying land in New Zealand began to prevail both in Australia and in England, and it being found that the natives would part with immense and most valuable properties for a few trifling baubles, they were cruelly imposed on by the class of land jobbers from the mother country. Thus Mr. Jameson writes (p. 274), "That an individual, representing a commercial firm in Sydney, laid claim to several hundred thousand acres, including the township of Auckland, for which he gave one keg of gunpowder."

The missionary operations both of the Church of England and of the Wesleyan community in New Zealand had now become very greatly extended; and in 1838 a Roman Catholic mission was founded in that country.

So little government was there at that time in the country, that in the year 1838 the body of settlers at Kororarika, in the Bay of Islands, met together and passed certain resolutions for the purpose of maintaining law and order among themselves, and in their transactions with the native community. These resolutions partook strongly of the character of "Lynch Law," and as it were to complete the picture, this infant community resorted more than once to the practice of tarring and feathering unpopular characters. Among other regulations made by the community of settlers, it was ordained that runaway sailors should not be harboured among them, but restored if possible to their lawful vessels.

The government in Great Britain had now for a considerable time past had the state of New Zealand under consideration, and it was resolved in the summer of 1839 to appoint a British consul there. This office was conferred on Captain Hobson, R.N., and that gentleman received instructions from the Marquis of Normanby, Secretary for the Colonies, who after mentioning that "a very considerable body of his Majesty's subjects have already established their residence, and effected settlements there (*i. e.* in New Zealand) and that many persons in this kingdom have formed themselves into a society, having for its object the acquisition of land, and the removal of emigrants to those islands," comes to the conclusion, that the most satisfactory way of terminating the state of anarchy which then reigned in those countries, would be " a voluntary recognition, if such could be achieved on the part of the New Zealand tribes, of the supreme authority of the British Crown over the island." He adds, " It is not, however, to the mere recognition of the sovereign authority of the Queen that your endeavours are to be confined, or your negociations directed. It is further necessary that the chiefs should be induced, if possible, to contract with you, as representing her Majesty, that henceforward no lands shall be ceded, gratuitously or otherwise, except to the Crown of Great Britain."

With these instructions Captain Hobson arrived at New South Wales towards the close of the year 1839, and after having had the oaths of office administered to him by Sir George Gipps, the governor of that colony, set out from Sydney and reached the Bay of

Islands the 29th of January, 1840. He at once issued an invitation to the British residents at Kororarika and its neighbourhood, to meet and consult with him, and sent an intimation of his wish to treat with the native chiefs of the Northern Island. On the 3rd of February an address was presented to the new lieutenant-governor from the great body of British settlers in that part of the country, admitting his authority and pledging themselves to do their best to aid him in establishing " order, law, and security for life and property in this improving and important colony."

On the 5th of February Captain Hobson, attended by all the most influential Europeans in that part of the country, met the native chiefs under a tent, and proceeded to explain the object of his mission, which was to induce them to recognise the supremacy of the Queen of Great Britain, and place themselves under her protection. At first this scheme was opposed with even violent language by many of the chiefs, one of whom named Rewa-Rewa said : " Send the man away; do not sign the paper; if you do, you will be reduced to the condition of slaves, and be obliged to break stones for the roads. Your land will be taken from you, and your dignity as chiefs will be destroyed." At a later period of the conference the Hokianga chiefs arrived, and these personages, being friendly to our government, quite turned the tide of feeling among the natives by their declamation. In conclusion it was intimated to the lieutenant-governor, that the body of chiefs were willing to sign the treaty with him, by which their independence was to be surrendered; and this was accordingly done on the following day at Waitangi, 512 signatures of native chiefs, (some of higher and others of lower rank,) being affixed to the document. A similar proceeding took place at Hokianga, the station of the Wesleyan missionaries, where Captain Hobson met several thousand of the natives. Great opposition was made here also; but ultimately all but two of the chiefs were induced to sign the treaty. Soon after these events Captain Hobson was seized with paralysis brought on by over fatigue, anxiety, and long exposure to wet.

On April 16th Major Bunbury arrived in New Zealand, and was forthwith despatched by the governor to visit in his name the most important parts of the Middle and Southern Islands, and endeavour to induce the native chieftains there likewise to recognise the supreme authority of Great Britain. Major Bunbury accordingly visited the harbours of Coromandel, Mercury Bay, Touranga, Hawke Bay, Port Nicholson, Robuka Island, the islands of Capiti and Mana, Otago, and Southern Port. "From all these places," he informs us, " I obtained the necessary signatures, excepting in two places, where my mission had been anticipated by other gentlemen sent by Captain Hobson. At Southern Port (Stewart's Island) and Cloudy Bay (Middle Island), Captain Nias and myself, judging it would be for the best interests of the natives as well as European settlers that further delay should not take place, we proclaimed the Queen's authority with the usual ceremonies; at the former place on the 5th of June, where we did not meet with natives, by right of discovery; and at the latter on the 17th of June, from the sovereignty having been ceded by the principal native chiefs." In this way was the sovereignty of the British Crown proclaimed in New Zealand. One of the chiefs, named Nopera, gave the following explanation of what had been achieved to his countrymen: "The shadow of the land goes to Queen Victoria, but the substance remains with us. We will go to the governor and get a payment for our land as before." Thus, as it has been aptly defined, the natives appear to have sanctioned the assumption, on the part of England, of magisterial jurisdiction only, with no intention of surrendering any of their territorial rights whatever.*

While these matters were being transacted, intelligence was brought to the lieutenant-governor that the inhabitants of Port Nicholson, a settlement formed by the New Zealand Company, had in a manner repudiated his authority as the emissary of the British government; that they had elected a council, and appointed Colonel Wakefield as president. Various

---

* See M. Martin, part xxix. p. 143.

other acts of authority which were considered to be illegal, as the raising of taxes, were moreover reported of this infantile community; and Captain Hobson, on duly weighing the matter, arrived at the conclusion that no time ought to be lost in proclaiming the authority of the British Crown over the northern part of New Zealand at least, and this he took care very soon to have done.

The government was shortly afterwards fixed at Auckland, a place very happily situated on a narrow isthmus of land some four miles broad which connects together the two extremes of the northern island.

Towards the close of this year, 1840, a charter was granted to the new colony of New Zealand, containing provisions for the erection of a legislative council of six persons nominated by the Crown, and an executive council, which was to be composed of three of the principal members of the government, to assist the governor with their counsel and advice. The governor was empowered to grant " waste lands " with this important restriction, however: " Provided always that nothing in these our letters patent contained shall affect, or be construed to affect the rights of any aboriginal natives of the said colony of New Zealand, to the actual occupation or enjoyment in their own persons, or in the person of their descendants, of any lands in the said colony now actually occupied or enjoyed by such natives."

A civil list was shortly drawn up which amounted to 19,300*l.*; this it was proposed to meet by 10,000*l.*, raised from duties levied on the soil of the new colony which had at that time a European population of about 4000; 5000*l.* were to be raised by the sale of land in the colony, and 5000*l.* was to be raised by a vote of the Imperial Parliament.

The New Zealand Company, to which allusion has been before made, was first called into being in the year 1837, Mr. Edward Gibson Wakefield bearing the principal part, both then and afterwards, in the history of its transactions.

This gentleman and his friends proposed to colonise New Zealand by the medium of an association of private persons formed at home, but on which it was hoped that the government would confer the stamp of approval, and perhaps grant a charter. It was to transact land sales to a large amount; and the colonists who went out under its fostering care, were to be recommended to amalgamate with the natives, and gradually train them to more civilised habits of life. Some of the schemes set forth for this purpose in a pamphlet by Mr. Wakefield were perhaps of too romantic a nature; and certain it is that the propositions of that gentleman and his coadjutors met with violent opposition on the part of the missionary bodies, both Church of England and Wesleyan, whose secretaries respectively made answer to his publication, in which the proceedings of the new company were discussed not always, perhaps, with courtesy.

In June 1837, the leading members of the Association had an interview with the Premier, Lord Melbourne, at which Lord Howick was present; it led to little or no result, however. In December of the same year, a deputation from the same company had another interview with the Premier, at which Lord Glenelg, the Colonial Secretary, was present; and these gentlemen were shortly after informed by Lord Glenelg, that though the government objected to its establishment by act of parliament, they would not be averse to granting a royal charter, by which the administration of the new colony should be placed for a term of years, in the company's hands.

During the session of 1838, a bill was brought into the House of Commons by Mr. F. Baring, for the colonisation of New Zealand by means of a private association; this bill was, however, through the influence of the government, thrown out by a large majority, and the hopes of Mr. Wakefield and his friends thus received a severe damper.

Nothing daunted, however, these gentlemen dissolved the "New Zealand Association," and formed themselves anew into a joint-stock company, under the name first of the "New Zealand Colonisation Company," but ultimately the "New Zealand Company." The government refused them any countenance, warned them against any land purchases in New Zealand, of which the validity might not afterwards be recognised by the Crown. They went on their course, however, and on May 2nd, 1839, issued a prospectus, in which it was announced that the capital of the company was to be 400,000*l.*, in 4000 shares of 100*l.* each; this was subsequently lowered to 100,000*l.*, in 4000 shares of 25*l.* each. The Earl of Durham was their Chairman, and there were several men of note among the directors of the company. An expedition was sent out in May, 1839, bearing agents of the company, who were commissioned to buy as much land as possible. This was done accordingly, and a vast territory, about the size of Ireland, lying north and south of Cook's Strait, was subsequently laid claim to by the New Zealand Company, for which they distributed in return a few thousand pounds' worth of baubles and implements of war, among the aborigines, who amounted, in that part of the country, to some thirty thousand in number. The proposals for land sales in lots were meanwhile caught at eagerly by the public at home, and several vessels full of emigrants proceeded, in 1837-40, to Port Nicholson, on the north side of Cook's Strait.

A commissioner, Mr. Spain, sent out by government to enquire into the validity of the land purchases made by the New Zealand Company and others, reports thus on the subject: "All the purchases of the company were made in a very loose and careless manner;" and subsequently he says, " I am of opinion that the greater portion of the land claimed by the company in the Port Nicholson and Wanganui, including the latter place, has not been alienated by the natives to the New Zealand Company; and that other portions of the same district have been only partially alienated by the natives to that body. . . . . . I am further of opinion that the natives did not consent to alienate their pahs, cultivations, and burying grounds."* The New Zealand Company, moreover, in several instances bought pieces of ground from the natives, which had been previously sold by them to missionary societies and others: in one case Colonel Wakefield took possession of a village which had arisen on land purchased by the Wesleyan community of Hokianga, with the view of instructing the natives in the neighbourhood of Port Nicholson. These facts seem to show, that the most humane as well as rational policy of the British government would have been at an early period of their intercourse with New Zealand to have claimed possession of the whole territory, and thereby prevented these endless quarrels which arose among its own subjects for the possession of small pieces of land; and furthermore shielded the ignorant inhabitants of the land from the gross deceptions practised upon them by the " civilised man."

* Parliamentary Papers, Nov. 19th, 1843.

It has been already mentioned, how the proceedings at Port Nicholson of the early settlers of the New Zealand Company had attracted the notice of Captain Hobson, and hastened the proclamation by the lieutenant-governor of the royal authority over the islands. These proceedings, which included the organising of a regular government in the new founded settlement, the levying of taxes, and the assumption of the right of jurisdiction even in cases of life and death, were pronounced unlawful by the most eminent legal authorities at home, and called forth severe censure on the part of the Queen's government.

Another important association was formed in France about the year 1840, principally by mercantile men of Nantes, Bordeaux, and Paris, which, under the name of Nanto-Bordelaise Company, sent out a vessel full of emigrants to Akaroa (Middle Island), their agents having previously gone through some transactions with the natives for the purchase of 30,000 acres of land in that neighbourhood, at a nominal price of course. The vessel in question, the "Comte de Paris," arrived at Akaroa, August 16th, 1840, escorted by the French frigate "L'Aube," Captain Lavaud. It so happened, however, that the officers of the British government had arrived just six days previously for the purpose of proclaiming the authority of Queen Victoria at Akaroa, a circumstance which was intimated to Captain Lavaud, who at once acknowledged the validity of the claim. The British government was ultimately induced to grant 30,000 acres to the Nanto-Bordelaise Company, and the matter was in the end settled to the satisfaction of all parties. This incident gave rise at the time to a rumour to the effect that the government of France contemplated just then the formation of a penal colony in the neighbourhood of Bank's Peninsula, a rumour of so groundless a nature, that it appears to have owed its invention to the sagacity of certain private individuals or companies, who had their own interests to forward thereby.

CHAP. V.

HISTORY OF NEW ZEALAND (*continued*).

In the month of August 1840 an Act was passed with reference to the possession of land in New Zealand by the authorities of New South Wales, in whose hands it will be remembered the government of the former country had been originally placed. In this Act, as in all others during the early years of our connection with New Zealand, there appears to have been too great hesitation on the part of government in claiming supreme authority over the entire territory and every part of it.

If this had been done, and if the authorities in England would have listened to the representations of Captain Hobson, who implored them to send him a few companies of soldiers to assist in keeping order over the country, great evils might have been avoided. The lieut.-governor, in a despatch to the colonial secretary in 1839, speaks thus: "No allusion has been made to a military force, nor has any instruction (been) issued for the arming and equipping of militia.

The presence of a few soldiers would check any disposition to revolt, and would enable me to forbid, in a firmer tone, those inhuman practices I have been ordered to restrain.* The absence of such support, on the other hand," he adds, "will encourage the disaffected to resist my authority, and may be the means of entailing on us eventually difficulties that I am unwilling to contemplate." The reply of the minister was to the effect that it was impossible at the present time to detach any of her Majesty's troops to New Zealand.

In the year 1840, an association was formed in the west of England, in connection with the New Zealand Company, to lay the foundation of a new settlement, to be called New Plymouth. The site of a town was ultimately fixed on the west coast of the northern island, in the neighbourhood of Mount Egmont. The first body of emigrants arrived there in the month of March 1841; they experienced many difficulties, and the progress of the colony was for a long time a very tardy one.

Towards the end of the year 1840, the British government came to the determination of granting a charter of incorporation to the New Zealand Company, at the same time requiring that a careful examination should be made of the transactions of that body, both at home and in the colonies. The terms held out to

---

* The offering of human sacrifices and cannibalism.

them were received with readiness by the company, whose interests, certainly, were not a little promoted by recognition from the Crown. The charter was granted on the 11th February, 1841. By its provisions the capital was fixed at 300,000*l.* in shares of 25*l.* each, two-thirds of which were to be paid up in twelve months' time. The company had power, moreover, to increase the capital to the amount of 1,000,000*l.*

In the year 1841 took place the formation of a third settlement on the part of the New Zealand Company at Nelson, on the south side of Cook's Strait, and almost opposite to Wellington. The company appear to have experienced great opposition on the part both of the natives and the agents of the missionary bodies with reference to the acquisition of land for this undertaking. In the same year (1841) the legislative council of the newly formed colony passed a Land Act, by which they repealed the decree of the government and council of New South Wales, enacted by them in September 1840, before New Zealand had become an independent colony. By the new law it was decreed that "all unappropriated lands within the colony of New Zealand, subject, however, to the rightful and necessary occupation and use thereof by the aboriginal inhabitants of the said colony, are, and remain, crown or domain lands of her Majesty, her heirs and successors, and that the sole and absolute right of pre-emption from the same aboriginal inhabitants, vests in, and can be only exercised by her Majesty, her heirs and successors." Moreover, all titles to land, whether "mediately or immediately," obtained from chiefs or individuals of the native tribes, were decreed to be absolutely null and void unless allowed by the Crown.

In May 1842 Mr. Spain arrived from England as special commissioner to consider and adjudicate the conflicting land claims in New Zealand; and shortly after Captain Hobson died at Auckland, his decease, it is to be feared, being accelerated by the increasing difficulties of his position as governor of New Zealand.

On the intelligence of this event reaching England, Captain Fitzroy, R.N., was solicited to take the post of governor, which he accepted. The affairs of the colony appear at that time (1843) to have been in the greatest confusion; the natives were on the point of taking arms to avenge their cause against the Europeans who had settled among them; while the latter were split up into small factions among themselves, the principal of these being the independent settlers, the missionaries and their friends, the New Zealand Company, and the whalers who lived here and there upon the coast, being for the most part runaway sailors and convicts, and many of them married to native women.

Governor Fitzroy arrived at New Zealand in the month of December 1843, and found everything in confusion. The Maories had risen against the agents of the New Zealand Company, and several of these, with Captain Wakefield at their head, had been shot down by them. During the month of August of the coming year 1844 the British flag, which had been raised at Kororarika, in the neighbourhood of the Custom House, was cut down by one of the native chieftains named Heké, who was accompanied by a party of armed men on the occasion. Ample apologies were made by several of his brother chieftains to Captain Fitzroy on his making inquiries into the affair, and the flag was restored to its place; but Heké repeated the hostile action during January of the year 1846. Our countrymen appear to have undervalued the courage and abilities of the natives of New Zealand; but their eyes were opened by some of the exploits which ere long followed.

Captain Fitzroy found the supplies of men and money for military operations so inadequate in the colony over which he was called to preside, that his hands were quite tied during the two years of his administration. At length, in 1845, he was recalled, and Captain (afterwards Sir George) Grey appointed governor in his place. The necessity was now seen for taking decisive measures against the hostile tribes, and the new governor was liberally supplied with the means of carrying on the war. It was not long before the steady discipline of civilised warfare dispersed these brave but savage enemies; some of their most influential chieftains were captured in the course of the year 1846, and hostilities gradually subsided between the two races.

Several promising settlements have been made of late years in New Zealand. In the year 1847, Otago was selected for this purpose by the New Zealand Company, and in 1850 the settlement of New Canterbury was set in hand.

During the last few years the Maori tribes have once more risen in arms, and afforded much trouble to our countrymen in New Zealand. They sustained a great defeat, however, towards the close of the year 1860, which it is hoped will render them incapable of committing any similar outrages for many years to come, perhaps for ever.

CHAP. VI.

ISLANDS OF THE SOUTHERN OCEAN. — DISCOVERY OF AN ANTARCTIC CONTINENT. — THE FALKLANDS. — THE AUCKLANDS. — THE CHATHAM GROUP.

THE amount of enterprise which has of late years been expended in the endeavour to penetrate the mysterious regions which encircle the South Pole, is very creditable to the spirit abroad on these subjects among the men of the nineteenth century.

The fleets of Great Britain, France, and the United States of America, have now established on a firm footing the existence of a vast territory, in all probability nearly as large as Australia, which surrounds the Antarctic Circle, and is itself enveloped almost entirely in perpetual snow and ice. A considerable number of islands and archipelagoes, some of which open out great resources as stations for those engaged in seal and other fisheries, while a few are pronounced to be not a little suitable for the establishment of European settlements, have likewise been discovered and investigated in the Antarctic Ocean. To several of these Great Britain possesses a claim, on what ground we will proceed to explain in the following pages.

THE FALKLAND ISLANDS.

This remarkable group or archipelago, consists of nearly 200 islands and small islets, and comprises an area of probably 6000 square miles. John Davis, an English navigator, discovered these islands in 1592; they were not however formally taken possession of by Great Britain until the year 1764, when Commodore Byron hoisted the national standard there. From that time nothing remarkable appears to have occurred with regard to the Falkland group until 1770, when the Spanish government determined to oppose the claim of that of England to their possession. So formidable a fleet was in consequence sent out from Spain to the Falkland Islands, that on its arrival at Port Egmont, the few British settlers, after a show of resistance, found it necessary to capitulate, and were ordered to depart. The intelligence of this event caused great excitement in England, and the Spanish government, in some alarm, tendered an apology for the violent measures used, and in fine offered to restore the settlement. This was soon after effected, and the British troops once more took possession of the Falkland Islands; they were abandoned, however, in 1774, the flag of England being alone left to mark its claim of possession; and for more than forty-six years from that period, they remained in great obscurity, being from time to time visited by ships engaged in the whale fishery.

In 1820 the South American patriots began to fix their eyes upon the Falkland Islands as a natural appendage to their vast continent, then rising so rapidly towards greatness and freedom. A faint attempt was made some years after, on the part of the government of Buenos Ayres, to obtain possession of the islands. A vigorous display, however, on the part both of Great Britain and the United States, caused them to cease from the warlike demonstrations, and on the 2nd January, 1833, the islands were once more taken possession of by a British force. In 1842 a lieutenant-governor was appointed by the imperial government, and the attempt was regularly set in hand to lay the foundation of a British colony in this distant region.

Of late years an important corporation has been formed, called the "Falkland Islands Company," whose principal object is to trade in the immense herds of wild cattle which have been multiplying in them from year to year since the period of their discovery. In 1849 the total population of the group was 300, of which all but three were whites. There are no aborigines inhabiting the Falkland Islands. It has been in contemplation to erect a convict establishment here, and the situation appears to be well adapted for the purpose on various accounts. On the whole the Falkland Islands have constituted a flourishing settlement of late years.

THE AUCKLAND ISLANDS.

This small group consists of one island of a large size and a few small islets. Its situation is in lat. 50° 48′ S., long. 166° 42′ E., and it is 180 miles to the south of New Zealand. They were discovered in 1806 by Captain Briscoe, and taken possession of in the name of the British Crown. In 1847 they were let on lease on the part of the Crown to the firm of Messrs. Enderby, of London, for the purpose of carrying on whale and seal fisheries in the South Seas. The firm in question has since sub-let their lease to the Southern Whale Fishing Company, with a capital of 100,000*l.*; and Mr. Charles Enderby has been sent out to the islands as commissioner of the company and lieutenant-governor of the islands. The population of whites in the Auckland Islands in 1851 amounted to 49 men, 19 women, 26 children, making a total of 94 persons; and as the climate is described as favourable to the inhabitants of the temperate zone, we may hope ere long to see a prosperous community rising among them.

Campbell Island, Macquarie Island, Antipodes Island, and the Bounty group of islets, are uninhabited, or only occasionally visited by whalers and sealers in the Antarctic regions.

THE CHATHAM ISLANDS.

These are a small group lying about 300 miles eastward of Cook's Strait. They were discovered November 23rd, 1791, by Lieutenant Broughton, R.N., and formally taken possession of in the name of his Majesty King George III. Nevertheless, the New Zealand Company in 1841 informed the secretary for the colonies, Lord Stanley, that they had acquired these islands by purchase from the natives, and it was their intention to sell them again to "certain parties officially connected with Hamburgh and other free cities of Germany." This statement was submitted by Lord Stanley to the law officers of the Crown, who informed him in reply that the conduct of the company in this matter was altogether unlawful, as interfering with the royal prerogative. The Chatham Islands were shortly afterwards constituted a dependency of the Crown, and placed under the charge of the Governor of New Zealand.

Chatham Island, the largest of the group, is about thirty-six miles in length. The climate is described as being stormy, but at the same time favourable to health. Some German missionaries have of late years been stationed on these islands.

SECTION VI.

THE REMAINING BRITISH COLONIES.

CHAPTER I.

HISTORY OF CEYLON, AND OF THE MAURITIUS, OR ISLE OF FRANCE.

THE celebrated island, known to the ancients by the name of Singhala, is situated near the extremity of the south-eastern coast of the Indian peninsula. It comprises an area of about 25,000 square miles, and contains many resources of different kinds, animal, vegetable, and mineral, which have not hitherto been adequately developed. Ceylon is one of the most ancient seats of civilisation among mankind, and in many parts of it are to be seen the relics of the art of past ages, some of them massive and stupendous in their character. Among these the most remarkable perhaps are the tanks or reservoirs of water, some sixteen miles in extent, composed of immense blocks of stone well hewn out, and bridges which display great artistic skill in their arches, canals and buildings which the traditions of the natives ascribe to a race of giants. Anuradpoora, the ancient capital of Ceylon, was founded about the year B.C. 437; its ruins are still traceable, and they prove it to have been of very great extent, and a list of its streets is said to exist at the present time. There are also to be seen cave or rock-hewn temples in Ceylon, similar to those of Western India. It may be doubted whether the modern world will leave behind it works of so stupendous and durable a nature as are witnessed in this small island of the Indian Ocean.

We do not possess many records of Singhala or Taprobane (its name with the Romans) in the ancient and mediæval periods of history. There is a curious Arabic work extant, which describes a visit of some Mussulmans of Western Asia to Ceylon and China; and Ceylon was visited in A.D. 1284 by Marco Polo, the Venetian traveller, and at a later date by Sir John Mandeville. The Portuguese began to have intercourse with the inhabitants of Ceylon after the commencement of the sixteenth century, and though opposed by the natives they managed to erect a fortress at Colombo (A.D. 1519-20). For many years they continued at this port, though continually at war with the Singhalese, but they were expelled from the island altogether by the rising power and influence of the Dutch republic about the middle of the seventeenth century. The Dutch, however, like their predecessors, though they held the coast line for the most part in their possession, were never able to extend their authority into the interior of the island.

Towards the close of the eighteenth century, the vast increase of the British Empire in India made it very desirable that our countrymen should obtain possession of Ceylon as a harbour of refuge, and an additional security in many respects to their power in the East. When, towards the close of the war of the American revolution, Holland joined with France and Spain in the "league of nations" against this country, the English authorities in the East made some ineffectual attempt to take possession, and Trincomalee was captured by Sir Hector Munro, but was restored in 1783, at the conclusion of the war. When, a few years after, hostilities had broken out on every side, and Holland, under the title of the Batavian Republic, had become in reality a mere province of revolutionary France, the English government once more attempted the conquest of the island of Ceylon towards the close of the year 1795. During this and the following year the sea coast of the island with the valuable fortresses of Trincomalee, Jaffna-patam, Colombo, and Galle, were wrested from the natives and the Dutch by a British force under General Stuart. The territory thus acquired was for some years made an appendage to the Presidency of Fort

St. George in Southern India, but in 1802 Ceylon was rendered entirely independent of the East Indian government. The Hon. F. North was appointed to the government in 1798, and appears to have taken every opportunity to get himself entangled in the intrigues which surrounded the court of the native sovereign at Kandy. It is with regret that we recount the sad consequences of this policy. Having quarrelled with the native government, Mr. North sent an expedition against Kandy in 1803, which not only failed in its object completely, but from gross mismanagement ended fatally, very few of our troops being left to record the tale. The rest were slaughtered with that barbarity which is but too characteristic of Oriental life and manners.

This dreadful cruelty was, however, destined to meet with a fit retribution; the King of Kandy became so notorious on all sides for his savage cruelty in after years, that the inferior chieftains of the island joined with the British government to dethrone him. Sir Robert Brownrigg at that time represented the British government in Ceylon, and as he considered the movement a salutary one, he joined the league formed against the native sovereign, who was captured on the 18th of February, 1815, and soon after dethroned, while the other chiefs declared their allegiance to the English government. For some years a very nondescript government continued to exist in

Ceylon, the English retaining supreme authority, while all inferior offices were held in the hands of natives; so that the Singhalese were still allowed, in great measure, the privilege of self-government. The priests and nobles, however, organised a conspiracy against the foreign domination of England; a pretender to the native throne was set up, and the standard of revolt was raised. During the first surprise of the insurrection, several individuals of high rank and authority among the English residents were slaughtered, and our troops suffered considerably during the ensuing campaign in a country and climate imperfectly known to them. The revolt was notwithstanding soon entirely subdued, and Ceylon was reduced to the rank of a British province; all offices being henceforth in the hands of Englishmen, or those appointed by the British government.

Under the rule of succeeding governors Ceylon has not failed to improve rapidly; very valuable public works have been constructed there, and ideas as well as habits of enlightenment are fast spreading among the body of the people; the commerce and physical resources of the island are constantly developing, and on the whole Ceylon may be considered as one of the most valuable possessions of the British Crown. The population of Ceylon in 1852 was given as 1,630,193, and it is said to be on the increase.

THE MAURITIUS, OR ISLE OF FRANCE.

This island is situated in the Indian Ocean, between lat. 19° and 20° South, and long. 57° 17' and 46° East; its area comprises an extent of some 676 square miles. It was discovered originally by the Portuguese navigators in the year 1507 A.D., and remained in the hands of their countrymen during the sixteenth century; in 1598 it was wrested from them by the Dutch, who named it Mauritius, in honour of Prince Maurice, the son of William of Orange, who was the great champion of their national freedom. For many years it was only held by the Dutch as a convenient situation for recruiting their vessels during the long voyages between Europe and the far East, and as a place of security. In 1648 some slaves were imported from the island of Madagascar; many of them, however, fled away ere long to the "bush," or uninhabited interior of the island, and having multiplied there in the course of years, they became a subject of great annoyance to the Dutch settlers, who abandoned the island entirely in the year 1712 to the "Maroons," as they are called. Shortly after this (1715) the Mauritius was occupied by a French force; and this step having been approved of by their government, it remained in the hands of France for several years, when it was transferred by the government to the French

East Indian Company, who retained it during a considerable part of the last century. For some years after its French occupation it remained a mere station for vessels during their long voyages round the Cape of Good Hope, while its inhabitants are stated to have been a collection of refugees and adventurers from every quarter of the globe. A great change was made, however, in the prospects of this little colony, by the appointment of M. de la Bourdonnais as governor-general in the year 1735. This remarkable person laid the foundation of that after career of prosperity, for which the Isle of France was formerly celebrated, but which a long course of disasters has since almost obliterated. On the breaking out of the great revolution this, like most of the other French colonies, thought fit to follow the example of their mother country in the career of change. A national assembly was convened, and clubs were instituted to watch its proceedings and overawe them in fact. After a few years a decree came out from the Assembly of France for the sudden and total abolition of slavery in their colonies; and this in the Isle of France, where out of a community of about 70,000 persons, 55,000 are stated to have been slaves, produced great indignation among the higher classes of the community. The result of these proceedings was a long and bitter struggle, which was only terminated finally by the triumph of the British arms, and the conquest by that nation of the Isle of France and its dependencies. Two expeditions were fitted out, one by the Marquis Wellesley in 1800, and another in 1810; it being at that time a great object of the English authorities in the East to hunt out that "nest of pirates of all nations," which was supposed to have accumulated under the flag of France at the Mauritius.

The expedition of 1810 comprised a fleet of twenty ships, bearing an armament of 12,000 troops, which had been despatched simultaneously in separate divisions from Hindostan and the Cape of Good Hope; they effected a landing near Port Louis, the principal town of the island, and after a few encounters the French capitulated. From that time the Mauritius has remained a British possession. Its population in 1851 was reckoned at 180,825, among whom every principal branch of the human family seems to have been more or less represented; 102,993 were stated to be of African descent, 72,236 of Asiatic descent, the rest were a mixed population of various nations, European and otherwise.

The Seychelles, Rodrique, and the Amirante Isles belong to the British crown, and are subject to the authorities who reside in the Isle of France. The Seychelles contain several valuable harbours, and may, on several accounts, hereafter become a valuable possession of the British Crown. They contain a population of somewhat under 7000 persons. In the event of an active trade arising between our own country and the eastern coast of the African continent, these islands will be very favourably placed as a station of call for various purposes to the vessels engaged in that service.

CHAP. II.

PULO PENANG. — MALACCA. — SINGAPORE. — HONG-KONG. — BORNEO AND SARAWAK. — LABUAN.

THE beautiful island of Pulo Penang is situated on the western coast of the Malayan peninsula; it is about sixteen miles in length, and twelve in breadth, containing an area of nearly one hundred square miles. This island appears to have been a century ago an uninhabited waste, covered with dense forests. In the year 1785 it was presented as a marriage gift to Captain Light, on that gentleman espousing a daughter of the King of Quedah, on the neighbouring mainland. By Captain Light it was subsequently handed over to the East India Company, who agreed to pay the King of Quedah a sum of 6000 dollars annually (which was in 1800 raised to 10,000) as a compensation for a tract of the mainland, along the sea-coast, which he had conceded to them. This tract was called "Wellesley Province," in honour of the then governor-general of India; it covers an area of about 140 square miles. The vegetation of Penang is of the most rich and varied description, comprising groves of the areka palm, from which the island takes its native name. There are two settlements, called respectively George Town and James Town, near the former of which is a fine harbour, which may hereafter prove of great service to the navies of Great Britain on occasion of any contest arising in the Oriental seas on a large scale. The population of the entire colony, including both the island of Penang and Wellesley province, was rated in 1853 at ₤1,098.

MALACCA.

This colony is situated towards the south-west coast of the Malayan peninsula, and contains an area of about one thousand square miles. The sea-coast is rocky and barren, and the interior of the country has a mountainous aspect. The climate is reckoned one of the healthiest in southern Asia, chiefly from its uniformity of temperature. The population of Malacca has been steadily on the increase for years past: in 1766 it only numbered 7216; in 1822 it amounted to 22,000; in 1853 it numbered above 50,000 inhabitants. The greater number of these are Malays and Chinese; there are a few thousands of Portuguese descent, and a sprinkling of the white race.

This settlement has passed through the hands of several European powers successively; the British government seized it from Holland in 1795, but restored it at the peace of Amiens in 1801. It was seized again on the breaking out of war, but once more restored in 1815. Malacca was finally obtained by England in the year 1825 in exchange for some settlements upon the island of Sumatra.

SINGAPORE.

This valuable British settlement lies at the very extremity of the Malayan peninsula; it contains an area of about two hundred and seventy-five square miles, and some fifty small islets are scattered through the straits in its neighbourhood.

The settlement of Singapore was originally undertaken on the design of Sir Stamford Raffles in 1818; the title of the British government to its possession was confirmed in 1825 by a convention entered into with the Dutch, and with the native princes of Jopore. At the time when it was taken possession of by England, it was the retreat of a nest of Malay pirates. The population of Singapore since the period of occupation has risen with great rapidity: from a few hundred savages it increased in three or four years to 10,688 permanent settlers, of whom ninety-four were Europeans. It is now about sixty thousand in all, including some thousand convicts. The climate is said to be not unfavourable to European constitutions. The administration consists of a Lieutenant-Governor, assisted by a small council, while a recorder performs a circuit twice a year through the colony for legal purposes.

HONG-KONG.

This small island lies off the coast of the Chinese province of Quang-tung, of which Canton is the capital; it is situated in 22° 16′ 27″ N. lat.; and 114° 14′ 48″ E. long.; and is about forty miles to the eastward of Macao. It belongs to a group of barren and rocky islands called the Ladrones, and is about eight miles long from east to west, while it is separated from the mainland by a narrow channel, which is found a convenient harbour for ships. The climate of Hong-kong is very unhealthy, principally from the damp and fetid atmosphere which is distilled out of the granite soil, after the heavy rains which fall during the summer months, not to mention the heat, which is intense at almost every period of the year.

The island of Hong-kong was fixed upon by the British commissioners who settled the articles of the treaty of Nankin in 1842, but experience has scarcely justified the expectations which were at that time made of its utility for political and commercial purposes. The mortality among the British troops who have been sent thither from time to time has proved excessive; and similar results, or even worse, have followed with the Hindoo sepoys.

The population of the island has increased at a very rapid ratio during the period of its occupation by the English; before that time it contained some 7000 inhabitants; in 1852 the population of Victoria, the principal town and seat of government, was 15,962, and that of the rest of the island 4,820, making a total of 20,782. Besides this, which only includes the Chinese population we believe, there are about 1000 Europeans and Americans, and many vagrants, besides a floating population who live in boats. "Altogether," says Mr. M. Martin*, "there are under 25,000 in the settlement; and not one respectable or wealthy Chinaman has ever fixed his permanent residence in Hongkong." This is not a very satisfactory account, it must be confessed!

The financial prospects of the colony are not of a very encouraging character, and it would appear upon the whole that, if England consulted her own interest, Hong-kong would be abandoned with as little delay as possible.

BORNEO AND SARAWAK.

The great island of Borneo occupies a central position in the Eastern Archipelago, and its importance, both in a political and commercial point of view, has long been recognised by competent judges. It is, next to Australia, the "island-continent," the largest in-

* Mr. Martin lately occupied a high official position at Hong-kong.

sular tract on the earth's surface, and doubtless contains within its vast territory numerous advantages in the animal, vegetable, and mineral kingdoms of nature respectively. It must be added, however, that hitherto little progress has been made towards the civilisation of the human race in this favoured region. The population is believed to comprise not much more than 3,000,000, and these principally of three different races, the Dyaks, the Malays, and the Chinese. The Malays established themselves in Borneo during the latter part of the fifteenth century, and subjected the Dyaks, who are (as far as we know) the aborigines of the island, to great hardship and persecution. The country has become parcelled out in later times among several independent sovereignties, and it is in a very abnormal state, by all accounts, both socially and politically. Several distinguished countrymen of our own have from time to time, from philanthropic motives, turned their attention to these regions, and set in hand various expedients for relieving the misery of the human race thereabouts. Two giant evils have afflicted the Eastern archipelago now for many years, not to say centuries; these are the practice of piracy, and that of a barbarous slave trade. The late Sir Stamford Raffles was very energetic in endeavouring to call the attention of the British government to these subjects, and others connected with the civilisation of the islands of the Malayan archipelago; but he seems to have been cut off early in his career. Another energetic friend of civilisation in these parts has been since produced in Mr. James Brooke, formerly a cadet in the East India Company's service, but who, having come in for a private fortune, fitted out a yacht, well armed and supplied with an efficient crew, in which he set sail for the eastern seas in December 1838 from England, and reached the ceast of Borneo in the following August. His arrival was hailed with joy by several of the sovereigns of the country, which was then almost in the last stage of disorganisation, and he was induced by the Sultan of Bruné (or Borneo proper) to accept the title of Rajah of Sarawak, with a grant of territory on the west coast of the island of which he was to be the ruler. This occurred in 1841, and some time after Mr. Brooke, whose proceedings had been favourably noticed in England, received the honour of knighthood, and was appointed by the English government consul-general and commissioner in Borneo, and governor of the island of Labuan off the coast, which he had himself induced the Sultan of Bruné to make over to Great Britain. From this time Sir James Brooke has seen his endeavours signally blessed. Piracy has been in great measure repressed in all these regions, and the same may be said of the odious slave trade. The population of Sarawak and of many other districts of Borneo, has very greatly increased in numbers and in all the comforts of social and civilised life. From 1500 inhabitants, Kuchin, the chief town of Sarawak, has risen in twenty years' time to 15,000, and the results with regard to trade and commerce are equally satisfactory. Missionary efforts have been commenced on a grand scale in Borneo, and a witness entitled to some credit, the late Bishop of Calcutta, has pronounced the Borneo mission to be the most promising on the face of the earth.

LABUAN.

The island of Labuan is situated six miles from the west coast of Borneo, in N. lat. 50° 19′, E. long. 115° 10′; it is about eleven miles in length, with a breath varying from seven to one mile; the whole area comprises some thirty square miles. The soil is of a good character, and the island was originally almost an entire mass of forest. The climate is healthy according to the tropical standard of health for northern constitutions. Labuan was ceded to the British Government in 1847 by the Sultan of Bruné; it contains at present a mixed population of some two thousand, consisting of Chinese, Hindoos, and Malays, with a few Europeans; it has a Lieutenant-Governor, who is assisted in his duties by a staff of inferior officers.

CHAP. III.

ADEN. — MALTA. — THE IONIAN ISLANDS. — GIBRALTAR. — HELIGOLAND. — CONCLUDING REMARKS.

THE town of Aden is situated on a rocky peninsula, which projects into the Straits of Babel-Mandeb at the south-western extremity of Arabia, in N. lat. 12° 46′, E. long. 45° 10′. The province of Yemen, in which it is situated, is celebrated by the Arabian historians for its fertility and other advantages; one of them informs us that "Yemen the blessed is a large and populous country, endowed with every blessing by the Almighty." The town of Aden itself is, however, situated in the centre of an extinct volcano, which gives it a singularly barren and desolate appearance. It was a place of considerable commercial importance in the reign of the Emperor Constantine, under the name of "Romanum Emporium." Since the fall of the Roman empire, it has constantly declined in wealth and prosperity, and when it came into the hands of our countrymen of late years, is described as little better than a squalid village, with the ruins of ancient splendour, in the shape of aqueducts, tanks, and other buildings, profusely scattered around.

Aden has of late years been fixed upon by the British Government, both for a commercial depôt, and as a coal station for the steamers which ply on the overland route between England and India. Accordingly, Captain Haines was deputed in 1838 by the Anglo-Indian Government to conclude a treaty with the native sultan, M'Houssin, for the transfer of Aden to Great Britain as a coal depôt and harbour. This gentleman found great difficulty in the execution of the task committed to him from the well-known treacherous and cruel character of the sultan. It was, however, accomplished, not without the use of force, in November, 1839, and Aden has since remained in the hands of Great Britain, and is a place of ever-increasing importance and prosperity. The population at present amounts to about twenty-four thousand, and is of a very mixed character. Its harbour is a very fine one, and its great natural advantages as a maritime stronghold have been forcibly set forth by the Hon. Caleb Cushing, an American writer, who says that " Aden is, even more than Gibraltar, a castle of nature's own construction."

MALTA.

This is a small island situated in the centre of the Mediterranean, about sixty miles southward of Sicily, in 35° 53′ N. lat., 14° 31′ E. long. It is about seventeen miles long, with a breadth of about eight miles, and contains an area of something under one hundred miles. The coast is generally steep and rugged, and the interior is supplied with soil from the neighbouring countries, so that every part of the island is said to be cultivated with the utmost care. Cotton is cultivated there, and has been largely exported thence. The climate is warm but healthy.

The importance of this small island as a military and naval station, and place of defence, has been recognised from an early period of history, and it has been successively occupied by the Phœnicians, the Greeks, the Carthaginians, and the Romans. On the decline of the last nation, and the dissolution of their empire, Malta became the prey from time to time of the barbarians of Northern Europe, and the Saracens of Asia and of Africa. The followers of Mohammed were driven out thence in A.D. 1090, by some Norman adventurers, after an occupation of about two hundred years. The island became subsequently annexed to the kingdom of Sicily. In the year 1530, the Emperor Charles V., who had taken possession of Malta, handed it over to the knights of the military order of St. John of Jerusalem, in perpetual sovereignty, together with the little island of Gozo adjoining, and Tripoli. During the two succeeding centuries that followed, the knights of this illustrious order rendered good service to all

Christendom by the valiant manner in which they defended Malta against the invasions of the Turks of Constantinople, and the piratical inroads of the corsairs of Northern Africa.

In the year 1565, the Turkish Sultan Solyman invaded the island with a great fleet and army, and a siege followed, in which great deeds of valour were performed on the part of the native garrison, led by the Knights of St. John. In the end the Turks were repulsed, to the great joy of all Christendom. At this period, subscriptions were made in all parts of Europe, and a fund was raised thereby, which contributed to the building of a new and strongly fortified capital to the island of Malta. To this town was given the name of La Valetta; its defences are of immense strength, and it possesses great resources for maintaining a long and heavy siege.

Malta was seized by the French under Napoleon in the year 1798, and from that time the reign of the Knights of St. John in that island came to a close. The dominion of revolutionary France appears to have been most distasteful to the Maltese, who rose in insurrection against their new masters, and besieged the French garrison, some six thousand strong, in La Valetta. In this contest, the inhabitants of Malta solicited and obtained the aid of Great Britain, in consequence of which the French garrison was compelled to surrender in 1800, after a siege of some two years' duration. The English now undertook a provisional government of the island, which was continued until the close of the war, when by the treaty of 1814, Malta was recognised as an appendage of the British Crown. Its administration consists at present of a governor and a council of seven, appointed by the Crown. The population of Malta and Gozo amounts to about 131,000 persons.

THE IONIAN ISLANDS.

The republic of the Seven Isles is a small insular territory off the western coast of Greece, consisting of seven principal islands, Corfu, Cephalonia, Zante, Sta. Maura, Ithaca, Cerigo, and Paxo, together with some smaller islets. They comprise an area altogether of 1,097 square miles.

These islands have in almost every period of history preferred the position of a dependent to that of a sovereign state. After the dissolution of the old Roman empire, they passed through the hands of a variety of masters during many centuries, and the population has sadly declined in every respect, intellectually, morally, and in the physical comforts of life, from the long course of disorganisation and oppression which they have endured thereby. Towards the end of the fourteenth century, the Corcyreans (the inhabitants of Corfu) placed themselves under the protection of Venice, and the Ionian Islands thenceforth generally remained subject to that republic, for a period of about 400 years. At the treaty of Campo Formio in 1797, France and Austria divided the territories of the Venetian Republic between themselves, and the former power took possession of the Ionian Islands. In 1799, Ionia was taken possession of jointly by Russia and Turkey; and was shortly after constituted a republic, called that of the "Seven Isles," and placed under the protectorate of Russia by the provisions of the Treaty of Amiens. Ionia was however transferred from Russia to France, by a secret arrangement made in the year 1807. In 1809 Great Britain, then in the full fervour of the war against Napoleon, took possession of all the Ionian Islands with the exception of Corfu, which was surrendered to her by the treaty of 1814. By the provisions of the treaty of 1815, the Ionian Republic was placed under the protectorate of the British Crown, and has remained so ever since.

The total population of the Ionian Islands in 1854, amounted to 229,163; the Ionians retain the physical features of their Greek ancestors in a remarkable degree. The government consists of a lord high commissioner, who is the representative of the British crown; a senate, composed of a president and five members; a legislative assembly of forty members, eleven of these being permanent, while the twenty-nine others are elected from the class of nobility in the several islands.

GIBRALTAR.

This ancient and celebrated fortress stands on a rocky promontory, which stretches out into the sea at the point on the south of the Spanish peninsula, forming with the opposite coast of Africa the entrance to the Mediterranean Sea. The promontory consists of a lofty rock which runs from north to south for a distance of some three miles, with a breadth of about half a mile generally; while its greatest elevation on the south side is 1439 feet above the level of the sea. The ancient name of Gibraltar was Mons Calpe, and together with the opposite promontory on the African coast, it formed the far-famed " Pillars of Hercules," for ages the " Ultima Thule " of maritime enterprise among civilised nations.

Gibraltar became famous in the long and sanguinary contests between the Christians and the Moors in Spain. It remained in the hands of the latter nation almost without interruption for more than seven centuries, and was finally wrested from their hands in A. D. 1462, by John de Gusman, Duke de Medina, Sidonia. From that time Gibraltar remained in the possession of the Spanish Crown until the year 1704, when England being at war with Spain, a fleet of ships under Sir George Rook was sent into the Mediterranean. Sir George formed the daring plan, on the 17th of July, of seizing the fortress of Gibraltar, which he accomplished in a few days' time, with very slight loss to the British forces, the Spanish commander, who had only 150 men under his command, considering it advisable to capitulate. From that time Gibraltar has continued in the hands of the British nation, to whom it has proved a most valuable acquisition. It has stood several severe sieges at various periods since the British occupation, particularly the celebrated siege of 1779–82, when General Eliot, afterwards Lord Heathfield, with a garrison of 5382 men, held it for three years against an overwhelming force of Frenchmen and Spaniards, and finally remained master of the situation.

The town of Gibraltar, which lies on the north-west side of the promontory, contains a population of some 15,000 inhabitants; the whole colony is governed by the military commander for the time being. A valuable depôt has been established here by British traders, and thus Gibraltar is found useful for commercial purposes while it is of the utmost importance as a military and naval station to Great Britain.

HELIGOLAND.

This is a small island, less than two miles and a half in circumference, situated in the North Sea, in 50° 11' N. lat., 7° 51' E. long., not many miles from the mouths of the Elbe and Weser. It has an eminence some two hundred feet in height, on which is situated the upper part of the town; the low land which lies beneath it is subject to the incursions of the sea, and this has greatly diminished the size of the island in the course of centuries. Heligoland was captured by a British force in 1807 from Denmark, and in 1814 it was formally ceded to the British government. The population is about three thousand, who are chiefly employed as fishermen and pilots. It has been much visited by the inhabitants of the northern countries of late years as a watering-place.

This little summary of our colonial history is now drawn to a conclusion: the world, we think, might be fairly challenged to furnish any equal display of energy perseverance, and varied talent to that which has peopled two great continents with the British family of mankind. It is not possible to look into the future and predict minutely the course of events hereafter, but it may be said with confidence, that if the Anglo-Saxon race remain true to itself and to its former characteristics, to none other is reserved a greater, and to none perhaps so great a destiny in the world's history. So long a career of prosperity could not, however, arrive without entailing in its train grave and manifold perils; and our eyes have been already opened somewhat to these, by the course of events of late in the New World. There we have seen the inevitable consequence of a community too rapidly growing in size, wealth, and population; that consequence has been its violent disruption, and the outbreak of a sanguinary intestine war, which at present, shows no probability of being assuaged. This is an occurrence of dread import in itself, and England may well take warning from it, and prepare to set her house in order, lest she also, like her sister of America, should be assailed unexpectedly by the firebrands of civil strife and war. And how may such a result be accomplished? Let the mother country lose no opportunity of supplying her colonies with every facility which may contribute to their development, political, social, and civil, and let her finally be prepared to grant them complete independence, whenever their growth has become sufficient for that end; and thus her colonies instead of proving sources of weakness, and in the end perhaps of ruin, will remain to all ages the grandest monuments of her long and successful career.

INDEX.

Africa, N. W. Coast, Sect. IV. ch. i. ii. pp. 188—202.
Apprenticeship system in Jamaica, Sect. III. ch. iii. p. 122.
Ascension, Island of, Sect. IV. ch. ii. p. 200.
Ashantees, Sect. IV. ch. ii. pp. 197—200.
Auckland Islands, Sect. V. ch. vi. p. 282.
Australia, history of, Sect. V. ch. i. pp. 224—226.

Barbadoes, history of, Sect. III. ch. iv. p. 128; description, p. 128; settlement of English in, p. 129; becomes a crown colony, p. 130.
Bay Islands, history of, Sect. III. ch. vii. p. 169.
Borneo, account of, Sect. VI. ch. ii. pp. 297—300.
Bourdonnais, M. de la, in the Mauritius, Sect. VI. ch. i. p. 290.
Brooke, Sir James, in Borneo, Sect. VI. ch. ii. p. 299.
Brownrigg, Sir J., Sect. VI. ch. i. p. 287.

Cape of Good Hope, Sect. IV. ch. iii. iv. pp. 203 222.
Cape Town, Sect. IV. ch. iii. p. 204.
Cayman's, account of, Sect. III. ch. vii. pp. 169, 170.
Ceylon, history of, Sect. VI. ch. i. pp. 284—288; ancient monuments in, p. 284; chiefs of, give their allegiance to Great Britain, p. 287; revolt of priests and nobles, p. 288; made a British province, p. 288.
Chatham Islands, Sect. V. ch. vi. p. 283.
Code Noir of Jamaica, its severity, Sect. III. ch. iii. p. 111.
Committee of Commons, on apprenticeship system, Sect. III. ch. iii. p. 123.
Cornwall County (in Jamaica), insurrection in, Sect. III. ch. iii. p. 116.
Cotton, Sir Willoughby, commands in Jamaica, Sect. III. ch. iii. p. 117.

Falkland Islands, Sect. V. ch. vi. p. 280.
Fantees, Sect. IV. ch. ii. pp. 197—200.

Gambia River, Sect. IV. ch. i. p. 188.
Gold Coast, Sect. IV. ch. ii. pp. 195—200.
Guiana, British, Sect. III. ch. vii. p. 171.
Guinea, Sect. IV. ch. ii. p. 195.

Hayti, revolt of blacks in, Sect. III. ch. ii. p. 112.
Honduras, history of, Sect. III. ch. vii. p. 166.
Hong-Kong, account of, Sect. VI. ch. ii. pp. 296, 297.

Jamaica, description of, Sect. III. ch. ii. p. 101; its native inhabitants, ch. ii. p. 102; arrival of Columbus at, ch. ii. p. 102; captured by England, ch. ii. p. 104; population of, in 1851, Sect. III. ch. iii. p. 127; emancipation of slaves in, ch. iii. p. 120; absenteeism in, ch. iii. p. 125; apprenticeship in, ch. iii. p. 122.

Kandy, King of Ceylon, Sect VI. ch. i. p. 287; deposed, ch. i. p. 287.

Malacca, account of, Sect. VI. ch. ii. pp. 294, 295.
Maroons, first appearance of, Sect. III. ch. ii. p. 104; insurrection of, ch. ii. p. 109; last insurrection, ch. ii. p. 112; sent to Nova Scotia, ch. ii. p. 113.
Mauritius, history of, Sect. VI. ch. i. pp. 289—292; occupied by Dutch, ch. i. p. 289; slaves introduced, ch. i. p. 289; occupied by French, ch. i. p. 289; effects of the French Revolution in, ch. i. p. 290; British conquest of, ch. i. p. 290.
Missionaries in Jamaica, Sect. III. ch. iii. p. 118.

Negroes, when first introduced into North America, Sect. I. ch. i. p. 22; into the West Indies, p. 21; into Jamaica, Sect. III. ch. iii. p. 103; emancipation of, ch. iii. p. 120.
New Zealand, Sect. V. ch. iv. v. pp. 255—278.
New South Wales, Sect. V. ch. i. pp. 226—232.
North, Mr., Governor of Ceylon, Sect. VI. ch. i. p. 287.

Osai Tutu Quamina, king of Ashantee, Sect. IV. ch. ii. p. 197.

Port Royal (Jamaica), earthquake in, Sect. III. ch. ii. p. 108.

Raffles, Sir Stamford, Sect. VI. ch. ii. p. 298; memorialises the British Government on the Borneo pirates, Sect. VI. ch. ii. p. 298.
Registration of slaves in Jamaica, Act for, Sect. III. ch. iii. p. 115.
Roderigue, island of, Sect. VI. ch. i. p. 291.

Sarawak, Sect. VI. ch. ii. pp. 297—300.
Seychelles, account of, Sect. VI. ch. i. p. 291.
Sierra Leone, Sect. IV. ch. i. p. 189.
Singapore, account of, Sect. VI. ch. ii. p. 295.
Slavery, abolition of, Sect. III. ch. iii. p. 119.
Slave trade, Sect. III. ch. iii. p. 115 ; Sect. IV. ch. i. pp. 184—188.
Sligo, Marquis of, Governor-General of Jamaica, Sect. III. ch. iii. p. 120.
Smyth, Sir J. Carmichael, in British Guiana, Sect. III. ch. vii. p. 175.
South Australia, Sect. V. ch. ii. pp. 237—242.
Southern Ocean, islands of, Sect. V. ch. vi. pp. 279—283.
St. Helena, Island of, Sect. IV. ch. ii. p. 201.

Tasmania, Sect. V. ch. iii. pp. 248—254.
Trinidad, history of, Sect. III. ch. iv. p. 143.

Victoria, colony of, Sect. V. ch. ii. pp. 233—236.
Victoria, Hong-Kong, population of, Sect. VI. ch. ii. p. 297.

West Australia, Sect. V. ch. ii. pp. 243—247.
West Indies, abolition of slavery in, Sect. III. ch. iii. p. 119.
Windward Islands, account of, Sect. III. ch. iv. pp. 132—143.

THE END

www.ingramcontent.com/pod-product-compliance
Lightning Source LLC
Chambersburg PA
CBHW030746230426
43667CB00007B/859